זְמַן לִתְפִלָה
THE TIME FOR PRAYER PROGRAM

BOOK 3: עֲמִידָה

TEACHER GUIDE

Hillary Zana and Dina Maiben

A.R.E. Publishing, Inc.
Denver, Colorado

HOT LINE NUMBERS

A.R.E. Publishing (800) 346-7779 arepublish@aol.com
Dina Maiben (732) 364-8431 MAZALBUENO@aol.com
Hillary Zana (818) 760-2527 hillaryz@doar.heschel.pvt.k12.ca.us

Published by:
A.R.E. Publishing, Inc.
Denver, Colorado 80237

© A.R.E. Publishing, Inc. 1999

All rights reserved. No part of this work covered by the copyrights hereon may be reproduced or copied in any form or by any means — graphic, electronic, or mechanical, including photocopying, recording, taping, or information retrieval systems — without the written permission of the copyright owner.

Printed in the United States of America
10 9 8 7 6 5 4 3 2 1

Acknowledgements

Grateful thanks to:

The Directors of Education and teachers of the following congregations for the willingness to test and offer comments on the pilot version of Book 3, and to their hundreds of enthusiastic students: Cantor Keith Miller, Kehillat Ma'arav, Santa Monica, California; Julie Lebenson, Temple Judea, Coral Gables, Florida; Sharene Johnson, Ner Maarav, Encino, California; Diane O. Samet, Temple Sinai, Denver, Colorado; Karen Weiss and Cantor Pamela Siskin, Congregation Beth Israel, West Hartford, Connecticut; Darlene Siegel, Shomrei Torah Synagogue, West Hills, California; Daniel A. Bender, Temple Emanuel School of Jewish Studies, Honolulu, Hawaii; Dina Maiben, Temple Shaari Emeth, Manalapan, New Jersey; William Cohen, Beth Shir Shalom, Santa Monica, California; Vanessa Ehrlich, Lakeside Congregation, Highland Park, Illinois.

Those who served on our Peer Review Committee and offered many valuable comments and suggestions on the program prior to publication: Dr. Shoshana Silberman, Consultant for the Auerbach Central Agency for Jewish Education, Philadelphia, Pennsylvania; Lori Abramson, Director of Education, Temple Sinai, Oakland, California; Rabbi Bernard M. Zlotowitz, Senior Scholar of the Union of American Hebrew Congregations; Cantor Arlyne Unger, Cantor and Educational Director, Beth Tikvah B'nai Jeshurun, Erdenheim, Pennsylvania; Dr. Lifsa Schachter, Professor of Jewish Education and Director of the Center for Jewish Education of the Cleveland College of Jewish Studies, Cleveland, Ohio.

Nili Shamrat of Heschel Day School, Northridge, California, for her corrections and suggestions for the Teacher Guide.

Joanna Livne, Oral Hebrew Language Specialist at Temple Shaari Emeth, Manalapan, New Jersey, for her thoughtful comments and suggestions on the language component of the program. Her considerable expertise and insights about teaching Hebrew language in a short time frame were invaluable.

Rivka Dori, Hebrew Language Instructor and Coordinator of the Hebrew Program at Hebrew Union College-Jewish Institute of Religion in Los Angeles, for her very careful and perceptive reading of each and every draft of the Workbook, and for her help, support, and encouragement throughout the development of the זְמַן לִתְפִילָה series. Any errors in this Teacher Guide and in the Workbook are not hers and will be corrected in future editions.

Our publishers, Rabbi Raymond A. Zwerin and Audrey Friedman Marcus, creative and innovative educators who are dedicated to producing the highest quality materials for Jewish education. Their insightful and invaluable contributions have enhanced the program at every step along the way. Their faith and support were evident throughout the development of this program, and their willingness to listen to their authors is a precious gift.

Finally, very special thanks are due to our families, who willingly endured and shared our struggles and supported us as we pursued this dream. Without their unwavering love and confidence in us and our efforts, זְמַן לִתְפִילָה would never have come into being.

Contents

Overview of the זְמַן לִתְפִילָה Program 7
Goals of the Program 7
Guiding Principles 8
Elements of Each Chapter 8
Structuring a Lesson 10
Teaching Hebrew Reading 12
Background on the Amidah 14
Using Book 3
    Introductory Chapter 17
    Chapter 1 23
    Chapter 2 31
    Chapter 3 38
    Chapter 4 43
    Chapter 5 49
    Chapter 6 56
    Chapter 7 61
    Chapter 8 68
    Chapter 9 74
    Chapter 10 81
Appendix 1: Name Verses 90
Appendix 2: Review Suggestions 94
Bibliography 96

This Teacher Guide begins with an Overview of the זְמַן לִתְפִילָה Program, and with important general information about Book 3. This general information includes: Goals of the Program, Guiding Principles, Elements of Each Chapter, Structuring a Lesson, Teaching Hebrew Reading, and Background on the Amidah. Specific information for teaching each page of Book 3 begins on page 17. Please read the introductory material before going on to the page by page instructions.

Overview of the זְמַן לִתְפִילָה Program

The זְמַן לִתְפִילָה program is designed for students who have completed a Hebrew primer and are not yet B'nai Mitzvah. It is geared to students in Grades 4 through 6. The program is designed to teach prayer literacy and Hebrew language, with a strong emphasis on Jewish concepts and values.

The זְמַן לִתְפִילָה program consists of four books to be used over a period of two or three years. These are:

Book 1: בְּרָכוֹת (*Blessings*) – This is a "Prayer Readiness" Workbook that reviews phonetic reading and Hebrew vocabulary while introducing the blessings for sensory experiences, mitzvot, and special times. This book is designed for students who have completed זְמַן לִקְרֹא or any other Hebrew primer.

Book 2: שְׁמַע (*Shema*) – In this Workbook the Shema and its blessings for both evening and morning services are covered, as well as the nature of God and the prayers אֲדוֹן עוֹלָם and אֵין כֵּאלֹהֵינוּ.

Book 3: עֲמִידָה (*Amidah*) – This third book in the זְמַן לִתְפִילָה program focuses on the central section of every Jewish worship service, the *Amidah*.

Book 4: תּוֹרָה (*The Torah Service*) – The Torah service is taught, along with chapters on יָתוֹם, עָלֵינוּ, קַדִּישׁ, and the structure of the service.

Book 1 and Book 2 should be completed in one year. Book 3 and Book 4 are to be used during the following one to two years.

Goals of the Program

The program contains three facets: prayer recitation mastery, prayer concepts, and Hebrew language. The specific goals are:

1. Prayer Fluency

Students will be able to read or chant the prayers that are taught.

2. Prayer Concepts

Students will understand the major themes and concepts of the prayers.

3. Prayer Text Analysis

Students will understand selected words in the prayers, particularly Key Words, which represent Jewish value concepts. Students will be able to locate familiar words and phrases in the prayers, and use these phrases to infer additional meaning.

4. Why Pray

Students will explore their own beliefs about God, religion, and prayer.

5. How to Pray

Students will learn synagogue skills and the choreography of Jewish worship.

6. Hebrew Language

Students will be able to comprehend selected Hebrew vocabulary and structures.

7. Hebrew Reading

Students will be able to decode (read phonetically) any Hebrew text with accuracy. They will be able to recite selected phrases and passages with fluency.

8. Jewish Cultural Literacy

Students will increase their level of Jewish knowledge about holidays, the synagogue, historical figures, and traditions.

Guiding Principles

1. Core Concepts and Key Words

Each chapter is centered around a major theme of the prayer being taught. This theme is summarized by the subtitle that appears under the chapter title, and is expressed in the chapter's Key Word.

2. Theology

The endeavor here is to put God back into the curriculum so as to encourage students to grow in their own understanding of God, belief, and prayer.

3. Hebrew Language Component

The Hebrew language component complements the prayer curriculum. When possible, the Hebrew vocabulary has been chosen to reflect the themes of the prayers. For example, the Hebrew words for doctor, רוֹפֵא/רוֹפְאָה, and additional medical vocabulary are taught in conjunction with the concept that God heals the sick, רוֹפֵא חוֹלִים.

While selected words from the prayers are taught, prayer transdlation is not a goal, since it leads neither to a greater appreciation of the prayers nor to natural acquisition of the Hebrew language.

Finally, the selection of language elements as well as the overall approach to language instruction are based on a solid foundation of research in second language acquisition.

4. Diversity

The program is based on an appreciation of Jewish diversity as reflected in the customs of various communities and movements. Students are taught that there are many differing, authentic ways for Jews to worship and believe.

Elements of Each Chapter

Key Word Analysis

Each chapter's Hebrew Key Word is explored in terms of both its literal definition and its conceptual meaning. A connection is often drawn between the word as a Hebrew vocabulary item, and its connection to the theme of the prayer.

Core Concept

Each chapter is centered around a major theme of the prayer being taught. Many times, a story about Mrs. Shapiro's class is used to convey the core concept. A typical Hebrew School class, with a wonderful teacher, they are probably a lot like your students. Some are bright troublemakers. Others aim to please. There are soccer players and new students. Mrs. Shapiro is the teacher we all aspire to be, the favorite teacher we remember from our own childhood. She has a great sense of humor, is always in control, has an answer to every question, and knows her material inside and out. The Mrs. Shapiro stories (the first story in Book 3 is on page 14 of the Workbook) present the theme of each chapter in an interesting, non-didactic format. The goal is for your students in identifying with Mrs. Shapiro's class, to enjoy learning the chapter's theme.

Phrase Reading

Most chapters include a דַף קְרִיאָה (Reading Page) which provides practice in Hebrew word and phrase reading. Additionally, through Chapter 3, these pages systematically review all Hebrew phonetic decoding. The phrases on each Reading Page are from the prayers taught in the Workbook. The goal of these pages is for students to move from accurate reading of single words to fluent reading of phrases. Additional reading practice is provided by independent seat work.

Prayer Text

The text is given in Hebrew, written with one phrase per line. A gender neutral English translation is opposite each phrase. Because the original Hebrew is not gender neutral, many times this translation will not be word for word accurate. It will, however, convey the meaning of the Hebrew. If there is more than one version of the prayer, it will also be given.

The Twelve Gates

In this section students compare multiple versions of a single prayer. The "Twelve Gates" was first introduced in Book 2: שְׁמַע (Shema). The title of the section comes from the following statement by Rabbi Isaac Luria, which appears on page 10 of the Book 3 Workbook:

There are twelve gates through which the prayers of Israel ascend into heaven. Each tradition has its own gate. Thus, each Israelite should pray according to his or her own tradition so as not to bring confusion into the higher realms.

In some chapters students explore the differences between the Ashkenazic and Sephardic versions of the prayer. Most often, the differences are between the Traditional and Liberal versions of the text.

Text Exploration

Students take a closer look at the themes, concepts, or literary elements of the prayer.

Hebrew Language Enrichment

The new and review Hebrew language vocabulary and language elements for each chapter are listed in this Teacher Guide at the beginning of each section that deals with that chapter. The Hebrew language sections in the Workbook include אוֹצַר מִלִּים vocabulary pages, grammar pages, and pages that drill vocabulary and structures. The Hebrew exercises are on interesting topics or contain humorous situations. They engage students, rather than merely asking for translations of words. The Hebrew language component of the Workbook is optional. If modern Hebrew language is not a goal of your school, or if there are time constraints, these sections may be omitted.

Prayerobics

These sections contain practical instructions for how things are actually done in a synagogue service, including the traditional movements for each prayer.

Yidbit

These pages feature fascinating facts that enrich and extend the main idea of the chapter.

Personal Prayer Parchment

The concluding page of each chapter contains a creative worship activity. This affective component of the Workbook enables students to respond personally to the prayer. The prayer is reprinted as it would appear in a congregational Hebrew Siddur; without English translation or line numbers.

Dictionary

The Workbook concludes with a dictionary of Hebrew Key Words and vocabulary. Words are listed in Hebrew. After completing each chapter, students should fill in the English translations. Words which were used in Book 1 and Book 2 of this program have been listed with their translations.

Structuring a Lesson

In order to maintain student interest, it is desirable to design lessons that contain varied types of activities. You may discover that using the Workbook one page after the next doesn't allow you to vary your lesson activities as much as you would like. If this is the case, feel free to jump around within the chapter, perhaps choosing to do a Hebrew language section as a breather between two discussion sections. However, be sure that you do not introduce the Hebrew language sections out of order, as each section reviews vocabulary and structures introduced previously.

A typical lesson might include:
1. Review of Prior Learning
2. Reading Drill
3. Prayer Text Study
4. Discussion
5. Language Work
6. Seat Work
7. Worship
8. Homework

An exploration of how to incorporate each of these types of activities follows.

Review of Prior Learning

Include review in each lesson (even the first). Review both Hebrew language and the prayers taught in previous lessons. Hebrew can be reviewed with an oral game-like activity or a brief flash card drill. Prayers can be reviewed by chanting those previously learned.

Prayers and blessings taught in Book 1 and Book 2 of this program should also be reviewed. Suggestions for linking this review to the concepts presented in Book 3 are found in this Teacher Guide in Appendix 2: Review Suggestions.

Reading Drill

For reading drill suggestions, see the section on "Teaching Hebrew Reading" on page 12 in this Teacher Guide.

Prayer Text Study

Students should be able to sound out each word in the prayer correctly. Fluent reading will come with many repetitions. Using melodies can enhance the students' enjoyment and appreciation of the prayers once they have mastered fluent reading of the text.

While this learning is by necessity rote and not imbued with a sense of spirituality, it is important to maintain some sense of the holiness and dignity of the material being studied. Use the Workbook for your rote learning and save the Siddur for worship experiences. Don't practice reading prayers backwards, or in any way that would further separate the practice from actual worship.

Discussion

Many sections in the chapters lend themselves to discussion about religious beliefs and the themes of each prayer. These include the Mrs. Shapiro stories, the many quotations from sources both traditional and modern, the Personal Prayer Parchment pages, as well as the many questions that allow students to state an opinion. Each lesson should contain some discussion. In keeping with the guiding principles of this program, all opinions should be treated with respect, and the teacher should make an effort to present various points of view. On a practical level, students often want to rehash the same discussion week after week, or persist in repeating a point that has already been made. In such cases, it is important to get the discussion back on track or to move on to another activity. Even a productive discussion can potentially take up more time than is available, and the teacher may need to restrict the time allotted.

Language Work

The Language Work sections include the אוֹצָר מִלִּים vocabulary pages, the grammar pages, and pages that drill vocabulary and structures. Students will not be able to learn the Hebrew language elements by simply completing these pages. You must orally introduce the new language and continuously review previously taught concepts. If you have orally introduced the concepts beforehand, many of the language pages can be done as independent seat work, with partners, or in small groups. Since the language pages are sequential, don't skip any of them (unless you are omitting the language component). If you discover that students have forgotten previously introduced material, it is necessary to go back and reteach those concepts.

In the limited amount of class time available in a supplementary school setting, it is unreasonable to expect students to achieve oral fluency in Hebrew, or to be able to express themselves in writing. Reading comprehension of simple passages and some oral language are attainable goals. If this is not a priority in your school, or if your time to complete this Workbook is very limited, you can use the Hebrew language pages for additional reading practice.

Seat Work

Explain several pages that students can complete on their own and have them work independently, in pairs, or in small groups. You may also give assignments for prayer reading that can be done independently or by pairs. For example, have students record their reading of a prayer, read to a teacher's aide, sing along with a tape recorded prayer, or read to a friend.

Be sure to have additional activities ready for students who finish their seat work early. These might be independent learning center games, ways for students to extend their language learning, art activities, or additional methods for drilling prayer fluency.

Worship

Meaningful worship is the goal of all of the drilling. Bear in mind that for many students the time spent praying in class might be their main exposure to Jewish worship.

You will want to create a special environment for worship. You may want to have a special location for prayer — perhaps your synagogue sanctuary, a special corner in your room, or a spot outside. Choose a time that will be conducive to prayer, such as the beginning of class, as a warm-up activity to bring the class together. Or, you may prefer to have the prayer service be a transition between two activities in the middle of the class session. Prayer could also be a concluding activity at the end of the day. Some schools have special times set aside for the entire student body to pray.

Use music to create a worship atmosphere. Use rituals to increase the feeling that this is a distinct activity. You may want to choose one or two different students to act as leaders. Students can be encouraged to wear kipot and tallitot. Make sure that you use correct "choreography" of prayer according to the custom of your synagogue. For example, students should know when (and why) we face east, stand, bow, or cover our eyes. You may want to use your congregation's Siddur for your service so that students will gain familiarity with it. There are special Siddurim designed for school use as well, with larger print and explanations added for students. In general, it is preferable not to put together a folder of photocopied prayers for worship, even though that would be convenient for students, since this detracts from the goal of acclimating them to using a Siddur for prayer. However, some teachers may want to create a personalized Siddur for students, including copies of the prayers and places for students to add their own thoughts and responses.

Homework

Whether or not you assign homework is a decision to be made by your school administration. If your students will be completing this Workbook in one lesson a week, homework is strongly advised. It will help them remember the Hebrew language and prayer reading they learn in school. In addition, you will be able to move more quickly through the Workbook.

Do not send the Workbooks home unless you have a backup plan for individuals who forget to return them. You may choose to keep several unused copies of the text at school and let students who forgot their Workbooks write their answers on notebook paper.

Teaching Hebrew Reading

By now, students are moving from the decoding of single words to fluent phrase reading, and finally applying all of these skills to the reading of full texts.

At the beginning of the school year, students will probably need to review the basic letters and vowels, as they may not have read any Hebrew over the summer. Begin with the Key Word Poster Cards and Vocabulary Poster Cards that accompany the זְמַן לִקְרֹא program (available from A.R.E. Publishing, Inc.). Place six to eight words on the board or in another place where the whole class can see them easily.

This first step builds an auditory-visual association. This is extremely important, because unlike English reading, the goal of which is to promote silent reading ability, Hebrew reading in a supplementary school is something that should always be done aloud. The teacher points to the first word and pronounces it clearly. The class repeats. Individual students should be called on to repeat the word individually. Continue in this manner until each word has been introduced.

Next, the teacher calls an individual student up and names one word from the list. Using a pointer, the child indicates the word and repeats it. The rest of the class repeats the word, unless an incorrect word has been indicated. By the group's silence, the student should know immediately that he or she has made a mistake, and should be given the opportunity to self-correct the error. Any student who repeats an incorrect word is either unsure of the word or is not paying attention. Repeat this procedure until each student has had a few turns, and the class as a whole is able to repeat the words appropriately. This second step creates an auditory-visual-kinesthetic association and leads to greater recall.

If the students learned the meanings of these words during a previous year, a third step allows them to associate individual words with their concepts. This step is particularly appropriate when Key Words from זְמַן לִקְרֹא are reviewed in a chapter's language work. The teacher provides a definition or translation for one of the words. For example, if the word list contains חַלָּה, חַג שָׂמֵחַ, בַּר מִצְוָה and עִבְרִית, the teacher should say, "Find the words that . . .

. . . you would say on Sukkot." (חַג שָׂמֵחַ)
. . . describes what happens when a boy turns 13." (בַּר מִצְוָה)
. . . names the oldest Jewish language." (עִבְרִית)
. . . describes what you would eat on Shabbat." (חַלָּה)

The fourth step is a test of mastery. One at a time, individual students should be called up to read several words at a time, or the entire list. The child points to each word, reads it, and the class repeats if it is read correctly.

Once students can complete these steps with words they know, repeat steps 1, 2, and 4 with complex words drawn from the Siddur that the students do not specifically know. School closets are often full of boxed flash cards from various commercial programs that can be used for this kind of activity. Because these are words that are unfamiliar to the students, they may need to review the process of breaking them down into individual syllables and reblending them as whole words.

The multi-sensory approach to phrase reading is similar to that used for individual word reading. While phraseology is a decoding skill, it also acts as a bridge between basic decoding and recitation.

Use a chart that has 4 to 8 complete Hebrew phrases written in large letters, one phrase per line. These phrases should be drawn from the דַּף קְרִיאָה (Reading Pages) in Book 3. If the words are unfamiliar to the students, allow them to practice blending the words individually.

Hold the length of the pointer under the first phrase and read it in a rhythmic, conversational manner (not word by word), while sweeping the arm through the air in an arc from right to left. The class repeats the phrase while also drawing an arc through the air from right to left. The direction of this arc is significant, as it reinforces the directionality of Hebrew reading. The teacher should note any child who has difficulty with the direction and provide immediate remediation. Repeat this procedure several times with the class as a whole, then ask individual students to perform individually, with the class repeating after them.

This technique creates an auditory-visual-kinesthetic association. Students hear the phrase while looking at it, creating an auditory-visual link. They then say it while looking at it and drawing an arc through the air with their arms. It is almost impossible to read in a choppy manner when moving one's arm in a smooth motion.

As students master this kind of gross motor activity, move from reading posters to reading from individual sheets at their desks, and ask them to make the arc on the page with their fingers. At this point, periodic reviews using reading games will keep their skills sharp without the need for more extensive drill. To assist students further with proper phraseology, each prayer has been broken down in the Workbook into individual phrases, one per line.

All students must be able to recite each of the prayer texts fluently. The following activities are useful in fostering this fluency. First, read one line aloud. Have the class repeat the line back. Do this for several lines, until you reach the end of a sentence. Then, repeat the entire sentence, and have the students read it back. Choose individual students to read the whole sentence. After several students have read the sentence, continue on to the next part of the prayer. Keep reviewing the previous sentences as you continue reading through the prayer.

Prepare flash cards with phrases that repeat themselves in many prayers, such as לְעוֹלָם וָעֶד. Drill students until they can read these phrases quickly, without sounding out letter by letter. When you find these phrases in a prayer, have students identify them.

Another technique is to alternate reading between the teacher and students. The teacher reads the first word in a passage, an individual student reads the next word. The teacher reads the third word, and a different student reads the fourth word. Continue until the passage has been read. As fluency improves, the teacher and each student can read two words at a time, and later three. For more fluent readers, divide the class in half, and have each half alternate reading.

Vary these activities by assigning students to be "teachers." The "teacher's" job is to say if individual students read correctly. Award points to the "teachers" if they are able to say that a line was read correctly, or if they can spot an error. The student who is reading should not be penalized for any mistakes.

Similar techniques work well with the דַּף קְרִיאָה (Reading Page) phrases.

Teach a melody to go with the prayer. Many congregations have cassette tapes prepared for their B'nai Mitzvah students, or ask the Cantor to record the prayers that appear in this Workbook. After you have read through the entire prayer once, read along with the tape. Stop and rewind as needed. This can be done as a listening center activity by individual students or small groups.

Have students record themselves on cassette tapes as they read the prayer. As you listen to the tapes, make notes of their mistakes, and review the difficult words and phrases with the whole class. This can also be done with a computer, particularly if the teacher has a laptop. The advantage to using a computer is that the students' reading can be saved in a dated file, including notes on their errors or progress.

With each prayer that is added to the students' repertoire, continue reviewing all previous prayers learned, including those learned last year. Give students a context for this review, either reading all the morning prayers in the correct order, or all the evening ones, the שַׁבָּת version or the weekday version. Alternately, you could read different versions of the same prayer, and explain when each is said.

Background on the עֲמִידָה

Book 3: זְמַן לִתְפִילָה of the עֲמִידָה Program focuses on the central section of every Jewish worship service. The עֲמִידָה is known by three distinctive names, each of which highlights a different facet of its character. Each of these is described more fully below.

הַתְּפִילָה: "The Prayer" — emphasizing its primacy within the framework of Jewish worship.

עֲמִידָה: "Standing" — describing the worshiper's posture during its recitation.

שְׁמוֹנֶה עֶשְׂרֵה: "Eighteen" — indicating the number of blessings contained in the original weekday version of the prayer.

הַתְּפִילָה: "The Prayer"

The importance of the עֲמִידָה in Jewish worship cannot be overstated. When the Second Temple was destroyed, the daily recitation of this prayer was considered the substitute for the Temple Service (עֲבוֹדָה). Gradually, it became lovingly known as the "Service of the Heart" (עֲבוֹדָה שֶׁהִיא בַּלֵב), an appellation recorded in *Ta'anit* 2a.

The עֲמִידָה makes every individual Jew the "high priest" of his or her own internal sanctuary. The act of silent recitation allows for total and private communion with God, and a number of ritual customs have developed over the centuries to enhance the meditative mood it engenders. In many places, worshipers who wear a *tallit* pull it over their heads during the silent עֲמִידָה, creating a kind of tent that is reminiscent of the original Jewish sanctuary, the Tent of Meeting. Similarly, many worshipers sway throughout their recitation of the עֲמִידָה, carving out a small private space within the synagogue's larger sanctuary.

Finally, as some scholars have noted, the phrases, cadence, and style found in the עֲמִידָה are reminiscent of the Psalms. And, like the Psalms, the texts simply and elegantly express our noblest ideals and aspirations.

עֲמִידָה: "Standing"

The posture assumed by the worshiper during the עֲמִידָה is of great importance. As the name of the prayer implies, it is recited in a standing position, but the ritual is far more formalized.

The image of the עֲמִידָה is that of presenting one's personal and communal petitions before the Divine Court. This is the image Rav Chanina draws for us, as reported by Rav Yehudah in the Talmud:

> The first section — this is like a servant who arranges praises for the ruler. The middle — this is like a servant requesting payment. The end — this is like a servant who takes leave after receiving payment from the ruler. (*Berachot* 34a)

Just as one would not slouch before an earthly ruler, the worshiper should stand straight with his or her feet together while reciting the עֲמִידָה. Bowing is also an integral ritual, although generations of scholars have cautioned against obsequiousness. Instead, bowing is done at set times during the עֲמִידָה, and as is the case in the presence of royalty, a formal entrance and exit are both *de rigueur*.

שְׁמוֹנֶה עֶשְׂרֵה: "Eighteen"

The עֲמִידָה is not a single, uniform prayer. Rather it is a long series of connected blessings, varying in number and text for different times and different days. For example, both the Shabbat עֲמִידָה and the one for Festivals contain seven blessings, but the weekday עֲמִידָה traditionally has 19 benedictions (18 in some Liberal versions). While this fluid structure can make the עֲמִידָה difficult for the novice to understand and master, its original purpose was to provide a structural framework for individual prayer. Armed with only a working knowledge of the benedictions and their order, the worshiper was free to utter prayers for personal concerns at specified places within the service. In this way, personal prayers were bound to those of the community as a whole.

The blessings within the עֲמִידָה can easily be divided into three sets. The opening set of blessings praise God, and the same three blessings are always used, although certain additions and deletions occur within the text depending on the season and the time of day. The three blessings in the closing set are blessings of thanksgiving. Like the opening set, the themes covered in these final three blessings are consistent, while the text contains some variations depending on the day and time.

The middle set of blessings, however, varies greatly. On weekdays, the middle section contains a set of requests, or petitions, while, on Shabbat and Festivals, these are replaced with a single blessing for the sanctity of the day. Other blessings are found within this section during the High Holy Days or on public fast days. This structure affords the עֲמִידָה a great deal of flexibility, and provides a mechanism for balancing personal prayer with communal worship. The chart below diagrams the basic structure of the עֲמִידָה.

The weekday petitions can be further subdivided into three subsets. The first four petitions deal with our spiritual needs. The next two petitions are requests for the fulfillment of our personal physical needs, and the final group centers on the national needs of the Jewish people. The petition section is then closed with a request that God hear and accept our prayers. The specifics of the weekday petitions will be discussed in greater detail in the Background Information for Chapter 5.

According to Abraham Millgram (page 104), the origins of the עֲמִידָה are difficult to ascertain, as its development began during the period of Persian rule in Judea, a time from which few documents have survived. The Talmud is the primary source of our knowledge concerning the development of the עֲמִידָה, but the information it provides is scanty and somewhat contradictory. According to *Berachot* 33a, the Men of the Great Assembly established the blessings and prayers, the sanctifications and *havdalahs* for Israel. However, in *Megillah* 17b, we read that "one hundred and twenty elders, among whom were many prophets, drew up the 18 blessings." What is known is that the עֲמִידָה was left in a

FIRST THREE בְּרָכוֹת	
Merit of our Ancestors	אָבוֹת
God's Powers	גְּבוּרוֹת
God's Holiness	קְדוּשָׁה

MIDDLE בְּרָכוֹת		
Rosh HaShanah	Shabbat Festivals	Weekdays
מַלְכֻיּוֹת זִכְרוֹנוֹת שׁוֹפָרוֹת	קְדוּשַּׁת הַיּוֹם	בַּקָשׁוֹת
Special Verses	Sanctifying the Day	12 or 13 Petitions

LAST THREE בְּרָכוֹת	
Service	עֲבוֹדָה
Giving Thanks	הוֹדָאָה
Peace	שָׁלוֹם

largely fluid state for a long period of time. This can be deduced from *Berachot* 33a, which notes that at various times certain passages were included in the עֲמִידָה which were subsequently deleted as circumstances changed.

The final redaction of the blessings and formulae of the עֲמִידָה took place under the leadership of Rabban Gamaliel at Yavneh after the destruction of the Second Temple. There the blessing formulae and their order were firmly established, as well as a general outline of the contents and key phrases of each blessing, but not necessarily the full texts of the prayers that have come down to us. According to *Berachot* 28b, Shimon ha-Pakuli set the order and arranged the wording for the 18 benedictions. Rabban Gamaliel then requested the addition of a benedictilon against apostate sectarians, such as the Judeo-Christians. This was composed by Samuel the Lesser.

While the framework of the עֲמִידָה today is essentially the one established at Yavneh, this prayer has continued to grow and adapt as circumstances have changed. For example, a shortened version of the עֲמִידָה known as הֲבִינֵנוּ was developed for emergency use when reciting a full עֲמִידָה might be dangerous. Similarly, a sort of repetition of the Friday evening עֲמִידָה was added during the third century in Babylon at a time when synagogues had to be built outside the city walls. Latecomers would customarily remain behind after the service to complete their prayers. Although the evening עֲמִידָה is not generally repeated, the addition of the popular and melodious מָגֵן אָבוֹת prolonged the service enough to allow latecomers to participate in reciting the שַׁבָּת evening עֲמִידָה, and to catch up with the congregation. Thus members of the community could avoid walking home alone, a very dangerous practice after dark outside the protection of the city walls.

While these additional options grew out of pragmatic concerns for safety, other changes in the עֲמִידָה text have been made for philosophical reasons. This is especially true of the twelfth benediction of the weekday עֲמִידָה. As noted above, this blessing was the last to be added at Yavneh, and grew out of concerns over the growing number of sectarians. Over the centuries, the text of this blessing has frequently been modified. Sometimes textual changes have been made by the orders of medieval Christian censors. At other times, Jewish authorities have instituted changes, such as shifting the emphasis from members of the early Christian sects to the apostates who acted as informers against the Jewish community. Since the Emancipation, many liberal thinkers have expressed ambivalence about uttering a blessing against their Gentile neighbors. Initially the Reform movement removed this blessing entirely from the service, reverting to the original number of 18 benedictions. More recently, the blessing has been reinstated in Reform liturgy, but in a vastly modified form.

Finally, the עֲמִידָה has been enriched by an introduction and a concluding paragraph. The introductory line (Psalm 51:17) was added by Rabbi Yochanan in the third century. Because the עֲמִידָה was designed to provide the opportunity for personal prayer, various personal concluding paragraphs were composed by the Rabbis. *Berachot* 16b-17a cites the prayers of 11 sages. The one most commonly printed was composed by the fourth century Rabbi, Mar bar Ravina.

Using Book 3

Introductory Chapter אֲדֹנָי שְׂפָתַי תִּפְתָּח

Core Concept: We Ask God to Help Us Use Our Speech to Offer Praise.

Key Word: lip, language שָׂפָה

Review Letters and Vowels:

א ב ג ד ה ח ט י כ ל מ ם נ ן פ צ ק ר שׁ ת ת
ִ וּ ֵ ֶ ָ ַ

Review Vocabulary Words (optional):

family	מִשְׁפָּחָה	my, mine	שֶׁלִּי
world, universe	עוֹלָם	Hebrew	עִבְרִית
of, belonging to	שֶׁל	the Jewish People	עַם יִשְׂרָאֵל

New Vocabulary Words (optional):

stand (masc. sing.)	עוֹמֵד	lip, language	שָׂפָה
stand (fem. sing.)	עוֹמֶדֶת	languages	שָׂפוֹת
grandma	סַבְתָּא	Ladino	לָאדִינוֹ
grandpa	סַבָּא	Yiddish	אִידִישׁ
tongue, language	לָשׁוֹן		

The activity on page 6 of the Workbook introduces the names of several world languages, most of which are Hebrew-English cognates.

New Language Elements (optional):
The construct form (*S'michut*) is used, but the concept is not formally analyzed.

COUNTRY		NAME OF LANGUAGE	
גֶּרְמַנְיָה	German	גֶּרְמָנִית	
רוּסְיָה	Russian	רוּסִית	
פּוֹלִין	Polish	פּוֹלָנִית	
אִיטַלְיָה	Italian	אִיטַלְקִית	
טוּרְקִיָה	Turkish	טוּרְקִית	
יִשְׂרָאֵל	Hebrew	עִבְרִית	

Page 2: Dear Students and Reading Page

Pass out the Workbooks. Have students read the letter to themselves and have each write his/her name on the Workbook. Tell them where to write their name (inside the front cover or at the top right-hand corner of the front cover are two possibilities). Reassure students that while they may have forgotten a great deal of Hebrew over the summer, the knowledge is hiding somewhere in their brains, and they should be able to recall easily what they once knew.

The Hebrew reading drill at the bottom of the page begins a basic phonics review that will continue through Chapter 3 of this Workbook. The letters and vowels reviewed on this page were chosen because they frequently occur and are not easily confused. Whenever two letters look alike, only one of the pair is reviewed. For example, the letter שׁ is reviewed, but not שׂ; בּ is reviewed, but not ב. Only three vowel sounds are reviewed, the, "ah," "ee," and "oo" sounds. A complete list of letters and vowels reviewed in this chapter is found on page 17 of this Teacher Guide.

For this first Reading Page, you will want to start simply as possible. Use felt letters or flash cards to review the letters and vowels. Adjust your pace according to how much the students appear to have remembered. Introduce this page to the entire class. If possible, listen to students read in smaller groups. Use the techniques described in the "Teaching Hebrew Reading" section beginning on page 12 of this Teacher Guide.

Page 3: Hitting the Mark

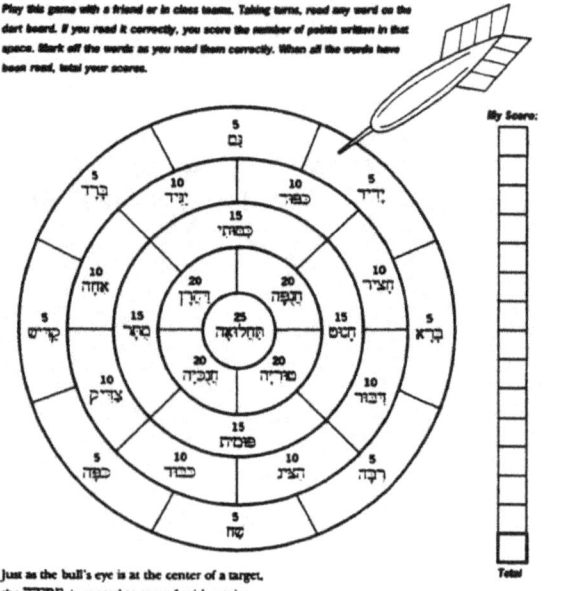

A review of basic phonics skills is contained in this game. Only the letters and vowels reviewed on page 2 of the Workbook are drilled in the game. Since you will not be able to judge for each group, words should be considered read correctly if both students playing agree on the pronunciation. While students are playing the game in pairs, walk from group to group listening in on their reading, and make note of any outstanding areas of difficulty, either with an individual's reading, or with that of the class as a whole. The game can also be played with two class teams. In this case, make a transparency of the page and use an overhead projector and erasable markers. Choose players from alternating teams to read the words.

Page 4: אֲדֹנָי מֶלֶךְ

The metaphor of the עֲמִידָה as similar to an appearance before a royal court is introduced here, and will be referred to throughout the Workbook. Each rung on the ladder represents a section of the עֲמִידָה in order. Read the opening paragraphs aloud with the class. Give students a couple of minutes to fill in their answers to the questions, and then ask if anyone wants to share his/her response. Since it is the beginning of the school year, students may feel uncomfortable sharing personal thoughts, or even writing them down. Now might be a good time to discuss how all ideas are welcome and will be treated respectfully, and the fact that they will find that many times in this program there are no right or wrong answers.

Page 5: אֲדֹנָי שְׂפָתַי תִּפְתָּח and Yidbit

Practice reading the Hebrew words with the entire class. Then read the line that introduces the עֲמִידָה (Psalm 51:17) until they can read it fluently. This line asks Divine help in using our power of speech to praise God. Conceptually, this verse and the ending paragraph of the עֲמִידָה (אֱלֹהַי נְצוֹר) form a set of bookends. Each deals with the concept of speech and its proper use. This concept is introduced here, but is not fully explored until the conclusion of this Workbook. However, it is important at this point to discuss the connection between the Hebrew language and Jewish prayer. This idea is summarized in the quote from Rabbi Yonatan.

While the Talmud cites a number of contradictory rulings, tradition has long held that prayer in Hebrew is superior to prayer in another language. Mishnah *Sotah* 7:1 declares that the שְׁמַע and the עֲמִידָה may be recited in any language. Conversely, Rabbi Yochanan declared that if one prays in Aramaic, the ministering angels ignore the prayer since they do not know Aramaic, and therefore may fail to transmit the prayer to God (*Sotah* 33a). Rabbi Abaye goes so far as to declare that secular subjects may be discussed in Hebrew, but sacred subjects may not

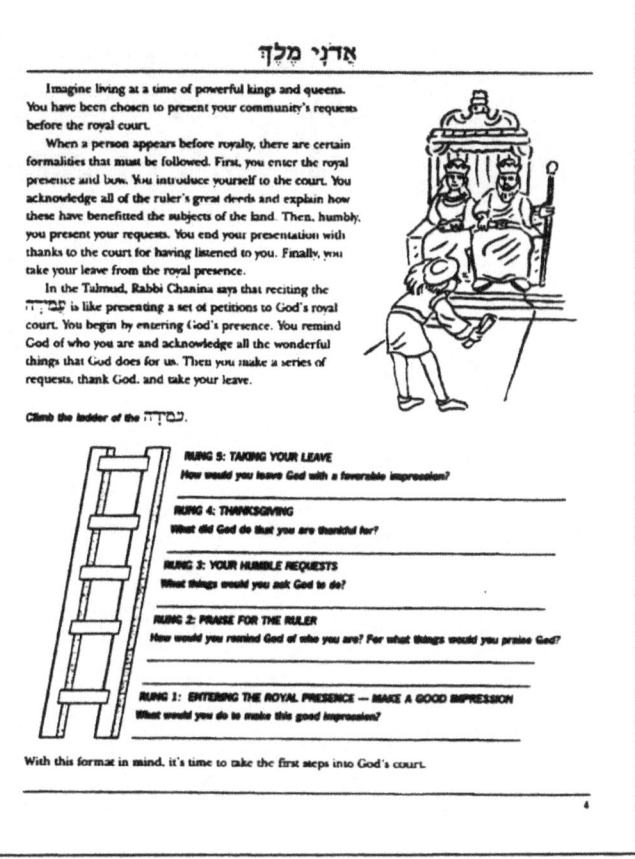

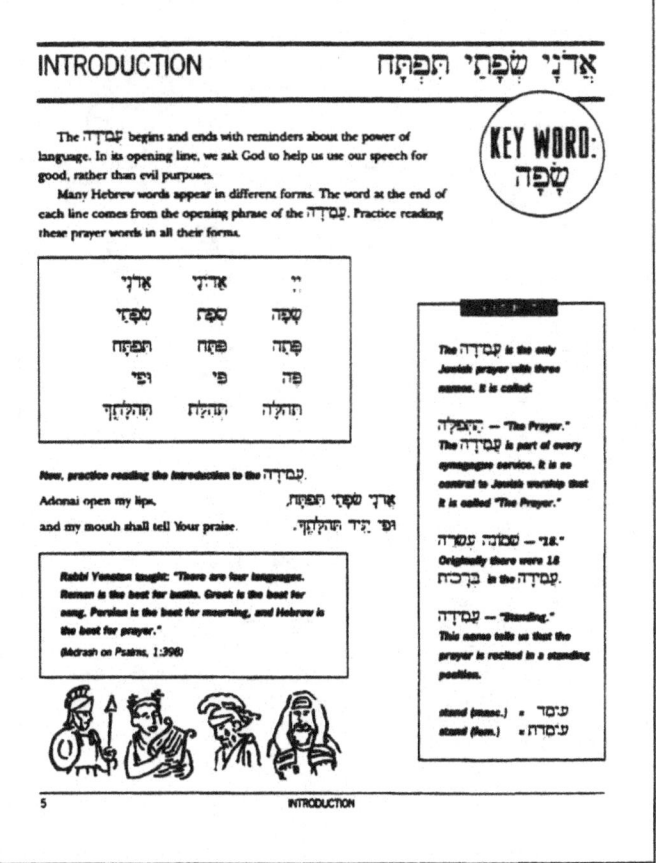

be discussed in any other language (*Avodah Zarah* 44b). And no less an authority than Maimonides emphasizes the maintenance of the Hebrew language as a means of insulating the Jewish people from foreign influences.

Languages in and of themselves often carry emotional associations that go far beyond their ability to convey information. For example, German often sounds militaristic, while Yiddish, despite its genetic relationship to German, lacks its emphatic stress and sustains a lilting and slightly mournful tone. To most Westerners, French sounds romantic, no matter what specific message is actually being sent. In such a context, Rabbi Yonatan's statement provides a glimpse at how the languages of the ancient world were perceived.

The Yidbit introduces the three names of the עֲמִידָה. These are discussed in detail in the Background on the עֲמִידָה section on pages 14 of this Teacher Guide. The verb עוֹמֵד is presented here, since it is related to the prayer's name. Later it will be used as new vocabulary.

Pages 6-7: Language Enrichment (optional)
הַשָּׂפוֹת שֶׁל עַם יִשְׂרָאֵל and הַשָּׂפוֹת שֶׁל הָעוֹלָם

These pages tie the chapter's concepts to a Hebrew language activity. Introduce the new vocabulary and cognates orally before using the Workbook. Use a map of the world or an atlas to identify the names of the countries in Hebrew while you are pointing to them. Ask students questions about languages spoken in their own families; personalizing learning makes it more meaningful.

Normally, after the preposition בְּ a *dagesh* would not appear in the letter פ as in the word בְּפּוֹלִין. However, in spoken Hebrew the names of places retain their pronunciation in spite of the rules.

Figurative usage is one of the oldest, richest, and most subtle forms of word building, and also the most flexible. It uses our brains' inborn talent for metaphoric thinking, for seeking patterns, and finding ways that two different items may be related. The Key Word שָׂפָה is an excellent example of how figurative use can extend the meanings of words for physical items.

שָׂפָה, the Hebrew word for "lip," has traveled from its basic meaning to represent language, something for which our lips are often used. Similarly, the English word "tongue" has also come to represent language, and the Hebrew word for tongue (לָשׁוֹן) has developed an identical figurative use. The אוֹצַר מִלִּים on page 6 draws the connection between the base meaning of שָׂפָה (lip) and its figurative usage (language).

To introduce the concept of figurative usage, ask students to brainstorm a list of figurative expressions in English. Some of these terms express emotional states. We speak of "feeling blue," depict jealousy as a green-eyed monster, and describe an unpleasant experience as "bitter." Other figures of speech are used for moral and intellectual concepts. We equate a straight line with being honest or true, and conversely use the term "crooked" to describe dishonesty. Likewise, we speak of making an arrow point or scoring a point in a discussion.

Interestingly, a great many figurative expressions cross over between Hebrew and English. In both languages מַר (bitter) describes a bad experience as well as a bad taste, גָּדוֹל (big or great) can describe a person's physical stature as well as his standing in the community, and תָּפַשׂ (grasp) applies equally to a tool and a concept in both languages.

Two distinct reasons at two different times in history account for this interesting exchange. First, the early Anglican Protestants believed that every word in the Bible was divinely inspired. When they translated the Bible into English, they did not want to tamper with divine writ, and so they tended to translate word for word. As a result, many Hebrew figurative expressions entered the English language at that time. Included on this list are יָשָׁר (straight/honest), as well as the three examples cited above.

The second cause is of more recent origin. As Hebrew has been revived as a modern language it has borrowed many figurative expressions from modern European languages. In this way, the ancient word שְׁאֵלָה (question) has also come to mean a problem, זֶרֶם (a stream) can be used as זֶרֶם הָעֲלִיָּה (flow of immigration) or זֶרֶם הַתּוֹדָעָה (stream of consciousness), תְּנוּעָה (a physical motion or movement) can also be used to describe an organization of people such as a religious movement (תְּנוּעָה דָּתִית) or a political movement (תְּנוּעָה הַצִּיּוֹנִית) or a youth movement (תְּנוּעַת נֹעַר), and נְקֻדָּה (a dot, spot, or point) has also come to mean a point in an argument or discussion.

הַשָּׂפוֹת שֶׁל עַם יִשְׂרָאֵל

Rebecca spent the summer with her grandparents. Grandma Mizrachi came to America from Italy and Grandpa Mizrachi came from Turkey. Both of them are Sephardic. In addition to speaking the languages of the countries where they grew up, they both speak Ladino. Ladino is a Sephardic Jewish language that developed from Spanish.

Isaac went to Europe with his grandparents. He was very surprised to discover that they could speak several languages. Grandma Klein grew up in Poland. Grandpa Klein was born in Russia, but moved to Germany as a boy. Both of them also speak Yiddish. Yiddish is an Ashkenazic Jewish language that developed from German.

All four grandparents studied Hebrew when they were young. They use their Hebrew whenever they visit Israel and as the Jewish language of prayer.

Draw lines to connect the people to the languages they speak in addition to English.

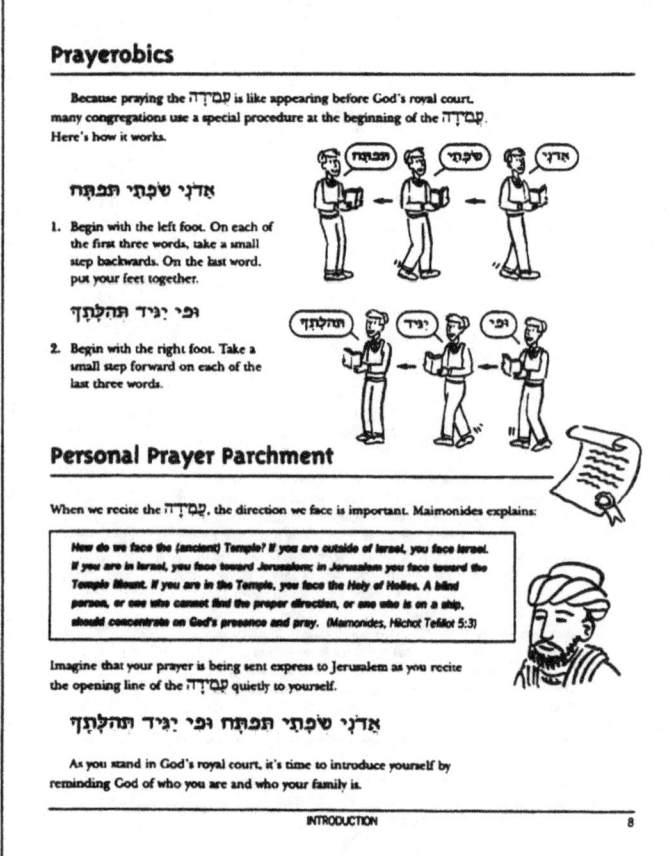

Page 8: Prayerobics and Personal Prayer Parchment

Demonstrate the correct body motions for the introductory line of the עֲמִידָה. With your back to the class, have students follow your lead, and practice enough times that they begin to feel comfortable with what will initially seem like a rather awkward dance.

After doing this, explain why all of you faced east. Tell students that many synagogue sanctuaries are built so that the congregation naturally faces Jerusalem. Sometimes a special sign marks the wall that faces in the direction of Israel. Because this custom developed in Europe, which lies to the west of Israel, this object became known as a מִזְרָח, meaning east. As a supplementary art project, students could create a decorative מִזְרָח for the classroom.

Students can read the page on their own, or refer back to it if they forget the correct steps and direction.

You can compare the procedures used at the start of the עֲמִידָה with those used when one appears before any royal court. Tell students that at the Wimbledon Tennis Championship, there is a royal box at center court. Only members of England's royal family may sit there. As the players come out to play, they follow a very formal procedure to acknowledge the presence of the royal family. First, they walk very straight and tall. As they reach a certain point, they stop with their feet together and bow.

Use this page as a preface to worship. Since the central concept of this chapter is language and the power of the tongue, you can teach the passage in Ameslan (American Sign Language), or another sign language. This will help students get more in touch with the emotional contents of this introduction.

Background Information

The עֲמִידָה is introduced by Psalm 51:17. This custom dates back to Rabbi Yochanan in the third century. It is not considered an interruption, but rather connects the עֲמִידָה to the גְאֻלָה blessing at the end of the שְׁמַע section of the service.

The reason for the selection of this text is most interesting. According to tradition, Psalm 51 was written by King David after he was confronted by Nathan the Prophet as penance for his affair with Bathsheba (see II Samuel 11 and 12). Since David's sin was willful, he was unable to bring a sacrifice as propitiation. Because the עֲמִידָה serves as a replacement for sacrifices, we add this verse in the hope that our prayer, like David's, will be accepted.

Chapter 1 אָבוֹת

Core Concept: Our God Is the God of Our Ancestors.

Key Word: patriarchs, ancestors אָבוֹת

Review Letters and Vowels:
שׁ צ ף פ ע ס ז ו ב יִ ִ ֵ ֱ (silent) ְ

Review Vocabulary Words (optional):

dad	אַבָּא	grandpa	סַבָּא	stand (fem. sing.)	עוֹמֶדֶת
mom	אִמָּא	grandma	סַבְתָּא	stand (masc. sing.)	עוֹמֵד
family	מִשְׁפָּחָה				

New Vocabulary Words (optional):

brother	אָח	uncle	דוֹד	father (formal)	אָב
sister	אָחוֹת	aunt	דוֹדָה	mother (formal)	אֵם
son	בֵּן	daughter	בַּת		

New Language Elements (optional):

The use of יֵשׁ is expanded to describe first person possession, (I have) יֵשׁ לִי.

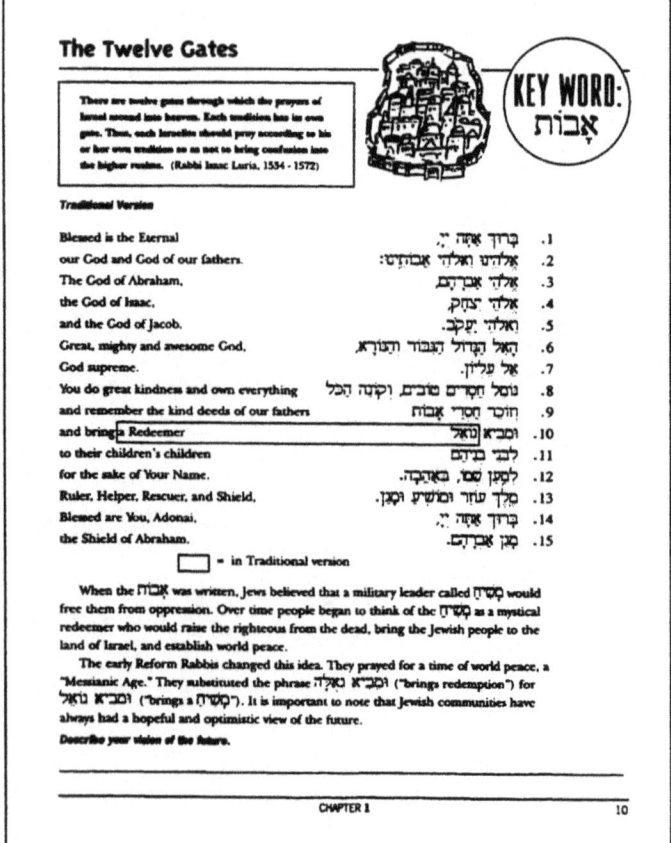

Page 9: Reading Page

Read the page with the entire class. This page reviews letters and vowels that can be confused with other items. For this reason, these concepts are reviewed after students have solidified their knowledge of the first item in the confusing pair. For example, כ was reviewed in the Introduction, and פ and ן are reviewed now.

The words at the top of the page also form an independent reading activity. All students should complete this activity, even if the class is not completing the optional Language Enrichment component of the Workbook. Even though students are asked to evaluate which word does not belong based on the meanings of the words, all of these words should be familiar to the students, as they include holiday vocabulary and names.

Once students regain a command of their basic decoding skills, they will need to work on fluent phrasing. To assist them in reclaiming this skill after a long summer vacation, phrases from the אָבוֹת prayer are drilled. These phrases should be practiced for fluency using the multi-sensory approach to fluent phraseology described above in the section on "Teaching Hebrew Reading" on page 12 in this Teacher Guide.

Pages 10-11: The Twelve Gates

The Twelve Gates pages in the Workbook compare differing texts and traditions, with respect for the different "gates" used in prayers by each community to reach God.

A comparison of Traditional and Liberal versions of the prayer text reveals two issues of controversy. These are the invocation of the Matriarchs along with the Patriarchs, and a belief in the coming of the Messiah.

According to tradition, the Patriarchs are all mentioned by name in the text to indicate that each of them had a separate, unique, and personal relationship with God. God affirmed the covenant with each of them individually. This is why the word אֱלֹהֵי is recited before each of their names. In contrast, the Bible records only one instance of direct communication between God and a Matriarch. Genesis 25:22-23 records the exchange between Rebecca and God concerning her twin sons. Because this is the only biblical citation of an exchange between God and a Matriarch, traditional versions of the text do not mention the אִמָהוֹת by name. Liberal versions of the text do invoke the Matriarchs by name in recognition of the changing status of women in the modern Jewish world.

While the inclusion of the Matriarchs is a recent occurrence, the controversy over praying for the arrival of a personal Messiah dates back to the very early days of the Reform movement in Germany. The early Reform Rabbis were opposed to any philosophical stance that was antithetical to citizenship in a Diaspora country. They systematically removed references to the reestablishment of a Jewish homeland in Israel from the liturgy. At the same time, they were greatly influenced by ratlionalism. As part of the European Enlightenment, they abhorred the mystical elements of Jewish tradition, since they considered them an obstacle to modernity. This was especially true of Messianism, as the havoc raised by false Messiahs was fresh in their memories. As a result, they removed references to a personal Messiah, and replaced this teaching with the notion of a "Messianic Age," a time of universal fellowship and perfection of the world. Students should understand that all Jewish groups see human history ending in an era of world peace. This contrasts strongly with the beliefs of many people in today's world that the ultimate fate of humanity is either nuclear or ecological destruction.

Teach the prayer with the melody used in your congregation. Have students do the exercise at the bottom of page 11 independently. Then ask: Has anyone checked off answers in both columns? Would it be acceptable to do so? What if someone's answers don't mesh with the practice at your synagogue?

In the current edition of the Conservative movement's *Siddur Sim Shalom*, a version of the prayer is given that includes reference to the Matriarchs, but with wording different from the Reform version. Teach this version if it is used in your congregation (see next page).

New Conservative Version of the אָבוֹת

Blessed is the Eternal	בָּרוּךְ אַתָּה יְיָ,	1.
our God and God of our ancestors,	אֱלֹהֵינוּ וֵאלֹהֵי אֲבוֹתֵינוּ:	2.
The God of Abraham,	אֱלֹהֵי אַבְרָהָם,	3.
the God of Isaac,	אֱלֹהֵי יִצְחָק,	4.
and the God of Jacob.	וֵאלֹהֵי יַעֲקֹב.	5.
the God of Sarah,	אֱלֹהֵי שָׂרָה,	5א.
the God of Rebecca,	אֱלֹהֵי רִבְקָה,	5ב.
the God of Rachel, and the God of Leah.	אֱלֹהֵי רָחֵל, וֵאלֹהֵי לֵאָה.	5ג.
Great, mighty and awesome God,	הָאֵל הַגָּדוֹל הַגִּבּוֹר וְהַנּוֹרָא,	6.
God supreme.	אֵל עֶלְיוֹן.	7.
You do great kindness and own everything,	גּוֹמֵל חֲסָדִים טוֹבִים, וְקוֹנֵה הַכֹּל,	8.
remembering the deeds of our ancestors	וְזוֹכֵר חַסְדֵי אָבוֹת	9.
and bring a Redeemer	וּמֵבִיא גוֹאֵל	10.
to their children's children	לִבְנֵי בְנֵיהֶם,	11.
for the sake of Your Name.	לְמַעַן שְׁמוֹ, בְּאַהֲבָה.	12.
Ruler, Helper, Guardian,	מֶלֶךְ עוֹזֵר וּפוֹקֵד	13.
Rescuer and Shield,	וּמוֹשִׁיעַ וּמָגֵן.	13א.
Blessed are You, Adonai,	בָּרוּךְ אַתָּה יְיָ,	14.
the Shield of Abraham and Guardian of Sarah.	מָגֵן אַבְרָהָם וּפֹקֵד שָׂרָה.	15.

Page 12: Language Enrichment (optional)
הַמִּשְׁפָּחָה שֶׁל רִבְקָה

The first person possessive יֵשׁ לִי (I have) is presented. First, introduce the concept orally by having students bring in and describe their own family pictures using phrases similar to the ones in the Workbook. You can model the language by describing your own family pictures. Go over the instructions with the students, making sure they understand how to complete the exercise. Then have students complete the page independently, in class or for homework.

The Key Word אָבוֹת is one of the richest words in the Hebrew language. Like the Key Word שָׂפָה from the Introduction, the Hebrew word אָב has been the source of figurative extensions that have traveled far from its original meaning, "father." Over the centuries, the term has also come to mean "primary," "source," "principal," or "chief," as in אַב-טִפּוּס or אַב-מִדָּה (prototype), אַב-הַטֻּמְאָה (source of pollution), or אַב-נֶזֶק (primary cause of injury), אַב-בֵּית-דִּין (chief justice, presiding judge or head of the Sanhedrin), אַב-מֶתֶג (master switch), and אַב-שָׁעוֹן (master clock).

Similar figures of speech have developed around the term "mother." These include אֵם הַדְּפוּס (matrix), אֵם הַדֶּרֶךְ (crossroads) לְשׁוֹן אֵם or שְׂפַת אֵם (mother tongue), and אֳנִיַּת אֵם (mother ship). Just as אָב can mean source, so too has אֵם come to mean source, as in אֵם כָּל חַטָּאת (root of all evil) and אֵם כָּל חַי (source of all life). Among the most charming examples of this use is the old Zionist appellations given to two important early settlements. Petach Tikvah was known as אֵם הַמּוֹשָׁבוֹת (the Mother of settlements), while the first kibbutz, Kibbutz Deganiah, was called אֵם הַקְּבוּצוֹת (Mother of collective settlements). In the אָבוֹת prayer, the terms אָבוֹת and אִמָּהוֹת refer to our ancestors. The basic terms for immediate family are introduced on page 12, and the connection of these terms to represent our forefathers and foremothers is made on page 13.

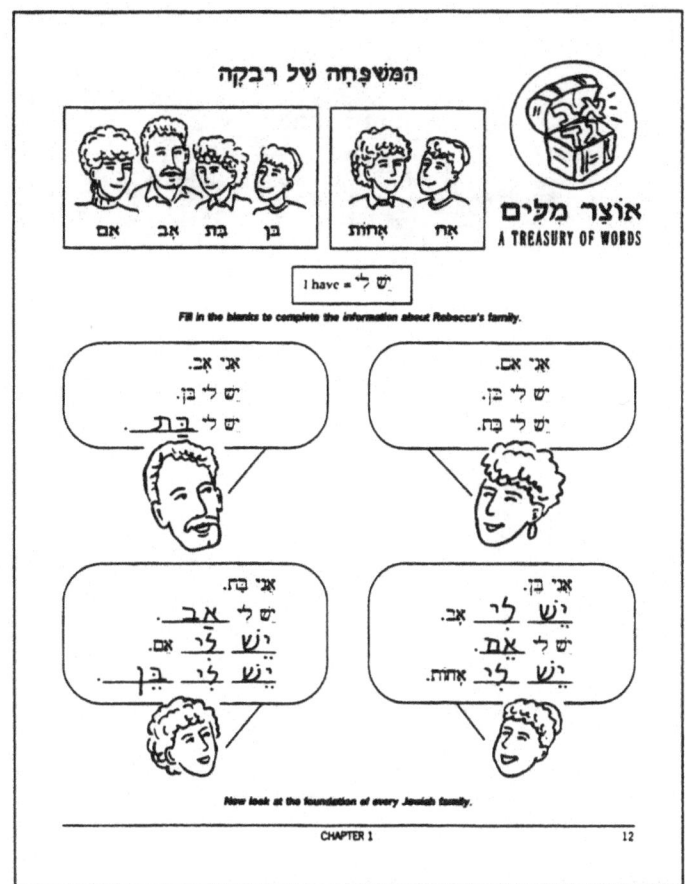

Page 13: Language Enrichment (optional)
אָבוֹת וְאִמָהוֹת

All students should be able to read the names in the family tree and understand the family relationships.

This Language Enrichment page connects the modern Hebrew vocabulary students have just learned with the theme of the chapter — the merits of our biblical ancestors. This is a good opportunity to review some basic knowledge of the lives of the Patriarchs and Matriarchs. The crossword puzzle should be completed independently in class or for homework.

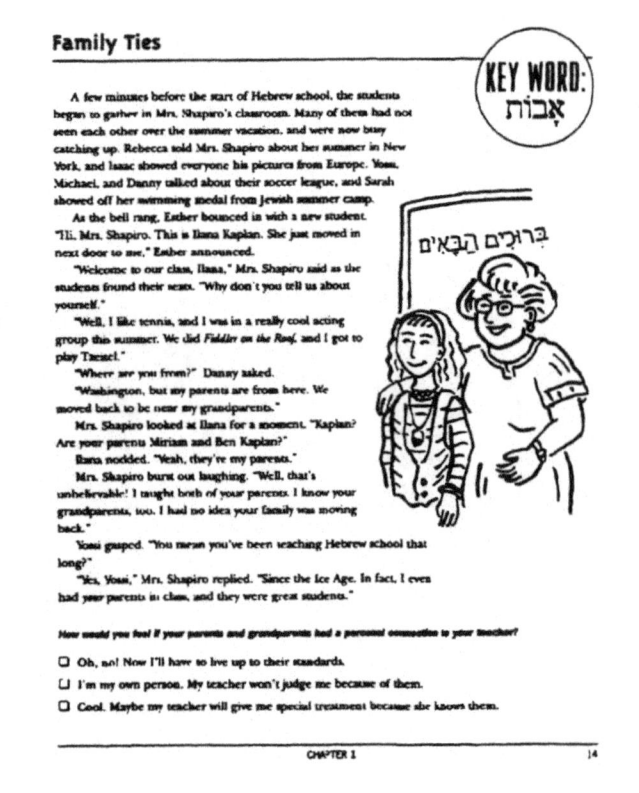

Page 14: Family Ties
In this opening blessing of the עֲמִידָה, we introduce ourselves to God by appealing to our ancestral connections. In Hebrew, this concept is known as זְכוּת אָבוֹת (Merit of the Ancestors). Even though we may lack a personal relationship with God, we present ourselves as heirs to the covenant established between God and each of our three partriarchs. Similarly, while we ourselves may be unworthy of the Almighty's attention, we base our appeal on the remembrance of our ancestors' kind deeds.

The theme of family connections is present throughout the chapter, and is linked to both the Hebrew language work and the review of biblical history.

Discuss the Mrs. Shapiro story with the class, then guide the discussion to the issue of the Jewish people's relationship with God. Who are our "grandparents" as a people? How will their deeds affect how God regards us? Do we need to live up to their standards, or are we entitled to special treatment?

Page 15: Language Enrichment (optional)
הַמִּשְׁפָּחָה שֶׁל אִילָנָה

This page provides practice in reading comprehension. First make sure that students understand the family tree drawing in English — i.e., what the solid and dotted lines represent. Have them translate דּוֹד and דּוֹדָה. Then orally give lots of Hebrew examples similar to the ones in the exercise. Finally, have students complete the exercise independently in class or for homework.

**Page 16: Prayerobics
and Language Enrichment (optional)
Where We Stand**

Physically demonstrate the body movements to the class and have students copy your movements. Initially, the motions may seem awkward and unconnected to spirituality for them. Later, when the movements become more natural, ask students if the motions add a dimension to their prayer experience.

The activity at the bottom of the page reviews the new verbs עוֹמֵד and עוֹמֶדֶת. Read all the sentences together with the students. Make sure they understand the meaning of all the vocabulary words by acting out or showing pictures, rather than translating. Students can complete the exercise independently in class or for homework.

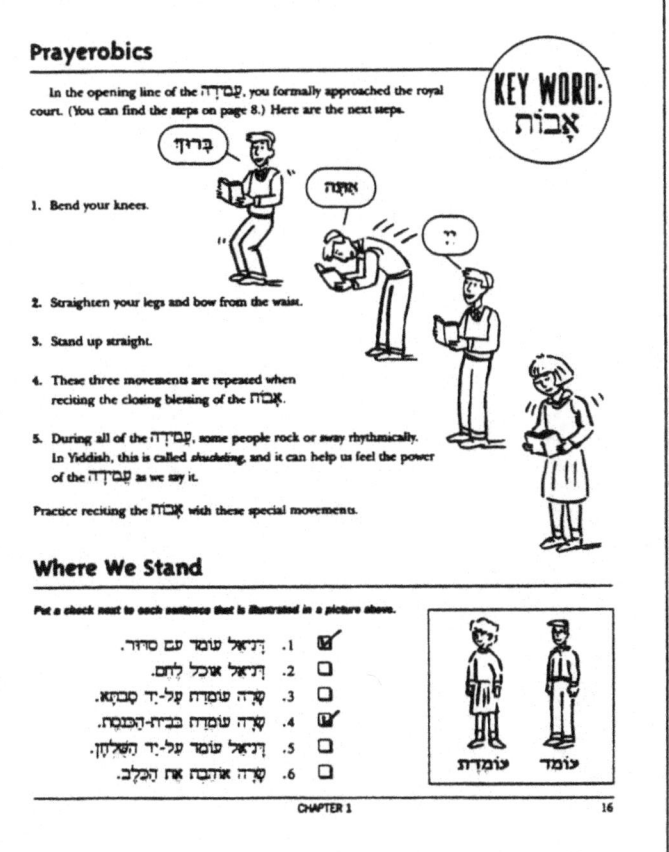

Page 17: Personal Prayer Parchment

Because the אָבוֹת centers on family and its connection to prayer, discuss those times that students have prayed with their families (including Seder experiences and synagogue services). How are these experiences different from school worship services? You may also ask students to read this prayer with their parents. In the latter case, provide a follow-up survey.

Students can complete the page independently. Give them the opportunity to share their answers before a class prayer service. Note that the prayer has been reprinted here without a translation, line numbers, or being divided into short phrases. This is done to help students transition into reading from a Siddur, and to provide another opportunity to practice reading without rereading the same page yet another time.

Background Information

During the High Holy Days, a line is added to this blessing which asks God to remember us and inscribe us in the Book of Life. This is true of both Ashkenazic and Sephardic liturgy, as well as for all denominational movements.

Chapter 2 גְּבוּרוֹת

Core Concept: Our God Is a Hero Who Works Miraculous Rescues.

Key Word: hero גִּבּוֹר

Review Letters and Vowels:

ץ ד כ חַ ◌ִי ◌ֲי ◌ָ ◌ֲ ◌ְ וֹ ◌ֵ (initial) ◌ְ

Review Vocabulary Words (optional):

dog	כֶּלֶב	grandma	סַבְתָּא
bird	צִפּוֹר	son	בֵּן
you (masc. sing.)	אַתָּה	student (masc. sing.)	תַּלְמִיד
you (fem. sing.)	אַתְּ	the students	הַתַּלְמִידִים
he	הוּא	teacher (fem. sing.)	מוֹרָה
she	הִיא	house	בַּיִת
no	לֹא	classroom	כִּתָּה
there isn't	אֵין	see (masc. sing.)	רוֹאֶה
where?	אֵיפֹה	see (fem. sing.)	רוֹאָה
who?	מִי	all	כָּל
aunt	דּוֹדָה	today	הַיּוֹם

New Vocabulary Words (optional):

hero	גִּבּוֹר	ill (masc. sing.)	חוֹלֶה
heroine	גִּבּוֹרָה	ill (fem. sing.)	חוֹלָה
doctor (masc.)	רוֹפֵא	hospital	בֵּית-חוֹלִים
doctor (fem.)	רוֹפְאָה		

Review Language Elements (optional):
Review of Hebrew possessives: שֶׁלָּךְ, שֶׁלְּךָ, שֶׁלִּי, שֶׁל

New Language Elements (optional):
Introduction of third person possessives: (hers) שֶׁלָּהּ and (his) שֶׁלּוֹ

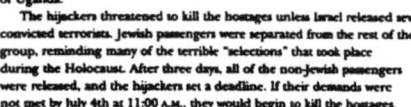

Page 18: Reading Page

The phonics review continues with this page. Read the words on the first eight lines with the entire class, or in small groups. These words are quite a bit more difficult than those reviewed in the previous chapters, and you should not be alarmed if students read rather haltingly. However, if you notice that some students are making many errors, without improving, these students may never have learned to decode correctly, in which case a cursory review will not be sufficient. You will need to analyze the situation to determine what the problem is. Perhaps the student has no reading difficulties, but has never completed a primer program. This might be a student who has received tutoring for reading problems in the past, or even a student whose serious reading problems were never detected. After talking with the child and evaluating the situation, inform your Director of Education of the problem.

Students can complete the circling of the Jewish biblical heroes names independently. Note that some Hebrew names appear on the lines that are not names of biblical heroes, such as חַיִּים on line 8. Also, any form of God's name is not a correct answer, since God, while a hero, transcends religious identification.

The phrase at the bottom of the page is drawn from the prayer text. Use the technique to teach fluent phrase reading found on pages 12 and 13 in this Teacher Guide.

Pages 19-20: Rescue at Entebbe

Several distinct concepts are interwoven into the text of the גְבוּרוֹת. One concept, expressed in both the chapter's subtitle and its Key Word, centers on God's unique ability to "snatch victory from the jaws of defeat." The story of the rescue of the hostages at Entebbe provides a modern illustration of this type of seemingly miraculous event — surely as profound a triumph of the few over the many in our own time as the Maccabean victory was in its day. Read the Entebbe story aloud with the class.

Page 20: Text Exploration
Page 21: גִּבּוֹרֵי יִשְׂרָאֵל

The Text Exploration activity introduces a second concept found in the prayer: God's heroism. The Almighty's power is a force for good expressed through heroic acts which are also well within human capability. Thus, the גְּבוּרוֹת serves to remind us of our responsibilities as God's partners in the world. The גִּבּוֹרֵי יִשְׂרָאֵל activity makes this point explicit, taking phrases used in the prayer to describe God's heroic actions and applying them to Jewish heroes. Students will need to refer back to The Text Exploration activity on page 20 of the Workbook for the translation of the Hebrew phrases.

The Key Word גִּבּוֹר means a "hero." Depending on context, the word can also mean "courage," "valiant," or "power." Although many people associate a גִּבּוֹר or a גְּבוּרָה (heroine) with acts of physical courage (as in גִּבּוֹר חַיִל), the prayer text gives us a very different definition of heroism. Here God is described as a גִּבּוֹר whose acts of heroism (גְּבוּרוֹת) include lifting the fallen, healing the sick, and freeing those who are captive. These actions may require physical courage, but at their heart lies a core of moral courage. Jewish tradition defines heroes and heroines as those whose acts have made the world a better place for others. In the Text Exploration activity on page 20, students are asked to examine various definitions of the word "hero" and to select the one that best defines the Key Word גִּבּוֹר. The גִּבּוֹרֵי יִשְׂרָאֵל activity on page 21 allows them to apply this definition to authentic Jewish heroes and heroines from our own time.

Begin teaching these activities with Workbooks closed. Have students give you the names of their personal heroes. List all the names on the board. Try to classify the characteristics that make them heroes (strength? talent? beauty?). Which of these characteristics actually defines a hero? Next, have students complete the two activities independently.

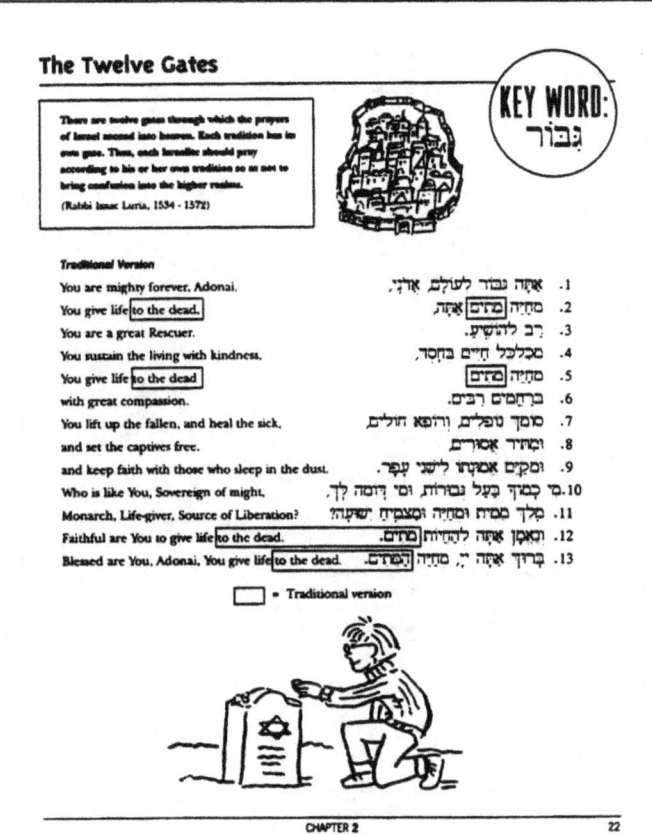

Pages 22-23: The Twelve Gates

Teach the prayer with the melody used by your congregation. The Understanding the Prayer Differences section at the bottom of the page 23 will lead to a discussion. All student views should be respected and seen as legitimate.

Collateral to the belief in a personal Messiah, resurrection of the dead has long been a traditional Jewish belief. Because of its mystical nature, the early Reform Rabbis eliminated all references to resurrection in the liturgy. The Twelve Gates activity provides students with an introductory exploration of eschatology, the branch of theology that deals with final things, such as death, judgment, and immortality. Grappling with these ultimate questions is necessary to the development of a healthy theology, no matter what beliefs the individual chooses to embrace.

Pages 24-25: Language Enrichment (optional)
אוֹצַר מִלִים

In Book 2, students were introduced to Hebrew possessives, including שֶׁלְךָ, שֶׁלִי, שֶׁל שֶׁלָך. This element is expanded here to include third person possessives (hers) שֶׁלָה and (his) שֶׁלוֹ.

Introduce the vocabulary and structures orally first. Collect objects whose names are known vocabulary from students. Ask: "שֶׁל מִי הַ___?" Students can answer using only names, for example: "David." Then model: "הַסֵפֶר שֶׁל דָוִד." Once this is understood and students can respond in a sentence, introduce the new structure, "הַסֵפֶר שֶׁלוֹ." Follow the same procedure to introduce the structure שֶׁלָה.

Have each student quickly sketch a picture of one of their parents and label it either, "name אַבָּא שֶׁלִי," or, "name אִמָא שֶׁלִי." Taking turns, have them hold up their pictures and chose a student to say either, "name אַבָּא שֶׁלוֹ," "name אִמָא שֶׁלוֹ", "name אַבָּא שֶׁלָה," or, "name אִמָא שֶׁלָה." Students that respond orally are allowed to be the next to hold up a picture.

Introduce the words חוֹלֶה and חוֹלָה with pantomine. Have students act out being ill as they say, "אֲנִי חוֹלֶה" or "אֲנִי חוֹלָה."

Next, open the Workbooks. Page 25 can be completed independently.

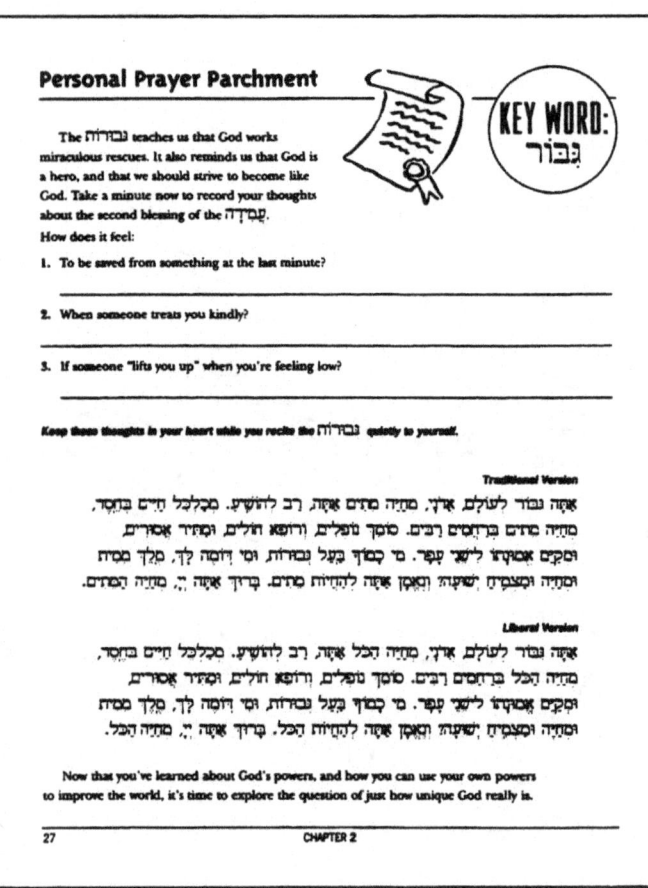

Page 26: Language Enrichment (optional)
מִי בַּכִּתָּה?

This page should be acted out. Two students can read the parts of Mrs. Shapiro and Yossi, and others pantomimine the activities of the absent students. The questions at the bottom of the page can be answered independently. Go over students' answers during the next lesson as a review activity for the new language items.

Page 27: Personal Prayer Parchment

As a lead-in to reciting the prayer, allow pairs of students to take turns role playing the following:

1. Lifting the fallen (Have one student lie down and pretend that he or she has fallen down; it is not necessary to require them to fall.)
2. Healing the sick
3. Freeing the captive
4. Keeping faith with those who are no longer with us

Allow groups to perform for the class, and discuss how it feels both to perform these acts, and to be the beneficiary of them.

As an alternative, ask students to close their eyes and picture a real hero or heroine. (This should be done only after students have completed the activities on pages 20 and 21.) Use guided fantasy to help them explore their heroes' qualities and actions. Then allow them to recite the prayer with their thoughts about the nature of heroism fresh in their minds.

The questions on the page can be completed independently, and the answers shared before reciting the prayer.

Background Information

In traditional prayer books, an additional line is inserted after the opening statement between Shemini Atzeret and Pesach. In this line we ask God to send the wind and rain. The time frame is significant, as this is added during the rainy season in the land of Israel. In some communities, a line asking God for dew replaces it during the summer.

The reason for including the line in the גְּבוּרוֹת is most interesting. The Talmud describes the practice, and equates rainfall with resurrection:

The miracle of the rainfall is mentioned in the benediction of the resurrection. What is the reason? Rabbi Yosef said: Because it is put on a level with the resurrection of the dead, therefore it was inserted in the benediction of the resurrection. (*Berachot* 33a)

The Midrash (*Beraysheet Rabbah* 13:4) explains the concept by way of metaphor. Rain nourishes the earth, allowing new life to grow. This resurrection of vegetation is comparable to bringing the dead back to life.

Chapter 3 קְדֻשָּׁה

Core Concept: Our God Is Unique in All the World.

Key Word: holy, special, set apart קָדוֹשׁ

Review Letters and Vowels:
מְמַ/לֵל   ְִ וֹ = ָ ֳ = ָ

New Vocabulary Words (optional):
good appetite, bon appetit   בְּתֵאָבוֹן

Review Language Elements (optional):
Students are reintroduced to the concept of Hebrew root words,
with an emphasis on the root of the Key Word.
Review of first person singular possessive יֵשׁ לִי.
Review of Hebrew possessives: שֶׁלָּהּ, שֶׁלּוֹ, שֶׁלָּךְ, שֶׁלְּךָ, שֶׁלִּי, שֶׁל.

New Language Elements (optional):
Exploration of root word ק.ד.ש. with practice in root letter isolation.

Page 28: Reading Page

This page concludes the reading review. Note that the *kamatz katan* vowel, which looks like a ָ, is sounded as a וֹ vowel. At this point, students should be able to decode correctly any Hebrew word. Now the emphasis becomes gaining fluency. Reading drill is provided in this chapter and in the rest of the Workbook through words and phrases drawn directly from the prayer text being taught. Phrase reading is especially important, as the goal is now to increase reading fluency. Read the words and phrases together with students. Use the suggestions for reading practice found beginning on page 12 in this Teacher Guide. The circling activity can be done independently.

Page 29: Praying Like the Angels

Because the core concept of this prayer is difficult to explore, a more general prayer concept is introduced here, namely the notion that not all prayers ask God to do things. Students of this age group tend to think of prayer as a glorified wish list, and successful prayer a matter of getting what they desire. Contrary to this widely held belief, Jewish prayer can be classified into three categories: Praise, Petition, and Thanksgiving. Although all three classifications are contained in the עֲמִידָה, the Rabbis expressed a preference for prayers of praise. The first three blessings in the עֲמִידָה all praise God, and since the קְדֻשָׁה is a blessing of pure praise, this concept is explored here in the story.

Read the story together with the class. Ask them to state with which student's opinion they most agree. The activity at the bottom of the page can be completed independently. Volunteers can share their answers with the class.

Pages 30-31: The Twelve Gates

There are several different forms of the קְדֻשָּׁה, each of which is recited at specific times or for specific purposes. Here it is necessary to draw a distinction between Traditional worship forms and those of Liberal communities. In traditional settings, when the עֲמִידָה is recited silently and individually, an abbreviated form of the קְדֻשָּׁה is recited. This is the version used in every evening service, as the עֲמִידָה is not repeated in the evening. In traditional settings, a full קְדֻשָּׁה is recited as part of the reader's repetition of the עֲמִידָה during morning and afternoon services, and only when a minyan is present. A different version of the full קְדֻשָּׁה is recited during the Musaf service. In many Liberal settings, the distinction between the abbreviated and the full קְדֻשָּׁה can be drawn solely along time lines, with the abbreviated form recited communally in the evening, and the full קְדֻשָּׁה recited during the morning and afternoon services.

While the abbreviated קְדֻשָּׁה is uniform across denominational lines, there are some variations from community to community. The text of the full morning and afternoon קְדֻשָּׁה varies greatly across the congregational spectrum. In order to simplify matters, students are asked to compare the Liberal and Traditional Ashkenazi versions of the Shabbat morning קְדֻשָּׁה in the Twelve Gates section on pages 30 and 31. The abbreviated קְדֻשָּׁה used in both Traditional Ashkenazi and Liberal congregations is presented in the Text Exploration section on page 32.

The Liberal version does not contain any overt references to angels or the Messianic vision of a return to the Temple in Jerusalem.

Page 32: Text Exploration

Through the activity at the bottom of the page, students are given practice in isolating and identifying the Hebrew root. The Key Word קָדוֹשׁ is one of the most difficult Hebrew words to capture fully in English. It is most often translated as "holy," a word with negative connotations to preteens, implying a sort of super-religiosity. The words "set apart," "special," "unique," "sacred," "sanctified," "dedicated," or "devoted" more fully capture its meaning.

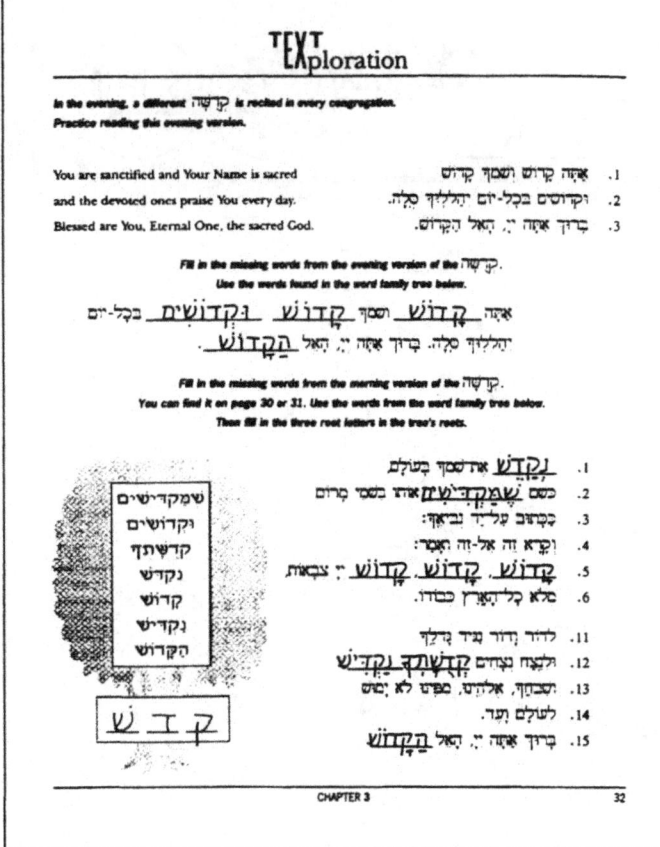

Page 33: Yidbit and Prayerobics

Read the Yidbit section together with the class. Students may be surprised about these Jewish ideas of angels.

Two different postures used while rising up on one's toes are presented in the Prayerobics section. Once students can easily recite the line that begins קָדוֹשׁ, קָדוֹשׁ, קָדוֹשׁ, allow them to practice it with the choreography, using first one posture then the other. Discuss the differences in the way each custom of reciting feels.

As the students begin to master the full קְדֻשָּׁה, you may wish to enrich their prayer experience further. The morning/afternoon קְדֻשָּׁה is based on three biblical texts (Isaiah 6:3, Ezekiel 3:12, and Psalm 146:10). The first, and most prominent, is Isaiah 6:1-8, which records Isaiah's vision of the Seraphim and Cherubim singing God's praises in the heavenly court. Ask students to read this passage and try to imagine seeing what Isaiah saw preparatory to reciting the full קְדֻשָּׁה.

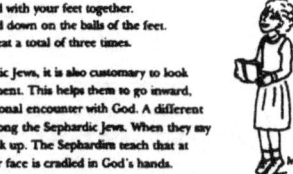

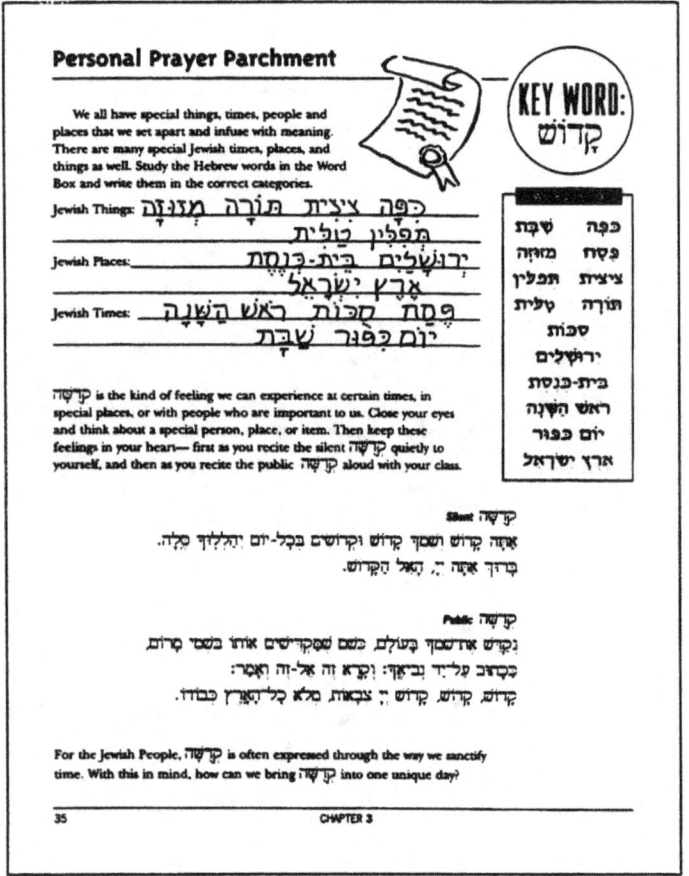

Page 34: Language Enrichment (optional)
אוֹצַר מִלִּים

This page reviews the possessive pronouns, particularly שֶׁלָּהּ and שֶׁלוֹ, which were introduced on page 24 in the Workbook. Use a similar activity to review the items as that described in the Teacher Guide instructions for page 24. This time, however, mimic the situation presented in the text, using brown paper bags with your students' names written on them and actual food items.

Page 35: Personal Prayer Parchment

The Personal Prayer Parchment explores the difficult concept of קְדֻשָּׁה. Although the unique and unknowable nature of God is central to the קְדֻשָּׁה prayer, this is a highly abstract and mature concept. To approach it in a manner that is accessible to students, the concept of קְדֻשָּׁה is explored through humanly accessible items (times, actions, places, etc.), which may be set apart for sacred purposes. Have students complete the page individually. Before praying as a class, ask for volunteers to tell about the special person, place, or item about which they have chosen to think.

Background Information

In traditional congregations, the text of the Musaf קְדֻשָּׁה contains a recitation of the שְׁמַע. Many scholars believe that this custom dates back to the reign of the Persian King Juzdegard II. In 456 C.E., he issued a decree prohibiting the recitation of the שְׁמַע. Government officials were stationed in synagogues during services to enforce the law. Refusing to give up the public recitation of the שְׁמַע, the Rabbinical authorities buried it in various parts of the service, so that it could be recited after the guards had left the synagogue. On Shabbat and festivals, it was placed in the Musaf קְדֻשָּׁה.

Although the ban lasted for only five years, the Rabbis retained the recitation of the שְׁמַע in the Musaf קְדֻשָּׁה to commemorate the event, and to publicize the miracle of their deliverance to future generations.

Chapter 4 קְדֻשַּׁת הַיּוֹם

Core Concept: Shabbat Is a Day Like No Other.

Key Word: Shabbat שַׁבָּת

Review Vocabulary Words (optional):

Days of the week:		of, belonging to	שֶׁל
Sunday	יוֹם רִאשׁוֹן	when?	מָתַי?
Monday	יוֹם שֵׁנִי	who	מִי?
Tuesday	יוֹם שְׁלִישִׁי	Hebrew school	בֵּית-סֵפֶר עִבְרִי
Wednesday	יוֹם רְבִיעִי	learn (masc. sing.)	לוֹמֵד
Thursday	יוֹם חֲמִישִׁי	to, for	לְ___
Friday	יוֹם שִׁשִּׁי	in the	בַּ___
Shabbat/Saturday	שַׁבָּת	grandpa	סַבָּא
Shabbat evening	עֶרֶב שַׁבָּת	grandma	סַבְתָּא

New Vocabulary Words (optional):

party	מְסִיבָּה	soccer	כַּדּוּרֶגֶל
go, walk (masc. sing.)	הוֹלֵךְ	drama	דְּרָמָה
go, walk (fem. sing.)	הוֹלֶכֶת		

Page 36: A Day Like No Other

Phrase reading to provide practice in fluent phraseology is provided. These phrases are drawn from the prayer texts. Use the techniques for fluent phrase reading described on pages 12 and 13 of this Teacher Guide.

The days of the week are reviewed later in this chapter of the Workbook on page 40. You can take the opportunity to go over them now.

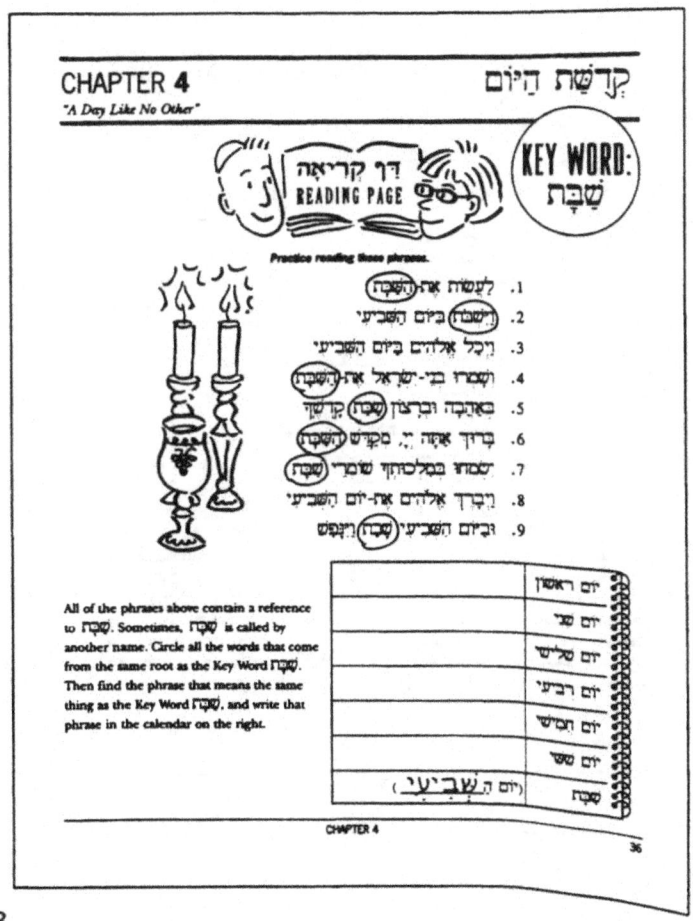

Pages 37-38: The Twelve Gates

As its name implies, the central idea of the קְדֻשַּׁת הַיּוֹם prayer is the notion that שַׁבָּת should be a day set apart. This concept is presented on this page and also through the Key Word activities on page 39 of the Workbook.

The blessing for שַׁבָּת is introduced by a short passage, which is the first passage on page 37 of the Workbook. While the text of the קְדֻשַּׁת הַיּוֹם blessing used in differing communities and denominations has only minor variations, the introductory passage varies greatly according to the time of day and the community. In traditional Ashkenazic congregations, וַיְכֻלּוּ introduces the blessing in the evening.

וְשָׁמְרוּ introduces the blessing in the morning service. It is the second passage in the Workbook, at the bottom of page 37.

יִשְׂמְחוּ introduces the blessing in the additional service for שַׁבָּת. This is the third passage in the Workbook, and is found at the top of page 38. In Sephardic congregations, יִשְׂמְחוּ is combined with וַיְכֻלּוּ in the evening and with וְשָׁמְרוּ in the morning. In Liberal congregations, יִשְׂמְחוּ may be used in the evening or the morning. It is interesting to note that יִשְׂמְחוּ is not recited in the afternoon service. The origin of this custom is the traditional teaching that Joseph, Moses, and King David all died on שַׁבָּת afternoon, and the aspect of joy is therefore tempered slightly at this time.

These pages should be done with the class together. Teach a melody for each passage. Students can answer the questions independently, in class or for homework.

Page 39: Crack the Code

Students at this age have certainly received a great deal of exposure to שַׁבָּת symbols and celebration, and have hopefully developed strong positive associations to the experience of שַׁבָּת. However, it is possible that their conceptualization of שַׁבָּת is based on early experiences during their primary years. If this is the case, their view of שַׁבָּת is likely to be on a fairly immature level. The goal of this page is to allow students to develop a more mature and sophisticated appreciation of the symbolic elements of שַׁבָּת celebration. Such comprehension is necessary for developing in them a deeper appreciation of Jewish culture, and it also keys into their emerging maturity.

The answers to the questions at the bottom of the page do not need to be based on a strict halachic interpetation. The concept is that everyday work and business should not be engaged in on שַׁבָּת. The goal is for students to perceive שַׁבָּת as a day of pleasure and relaxation. At this age, שַׁבָּת observance is almost completely dependent on the rituals and activities which their parents choose to practice. You can encourage students to do special activities on their own that would not be in conflict with their family's practices — for example, wearing favorite clothes, lighting candles Friday evening, or spending the night with friends.

The page can be done independently or as a pair activity. After students have answered the questions, have them share and discuss their answers.

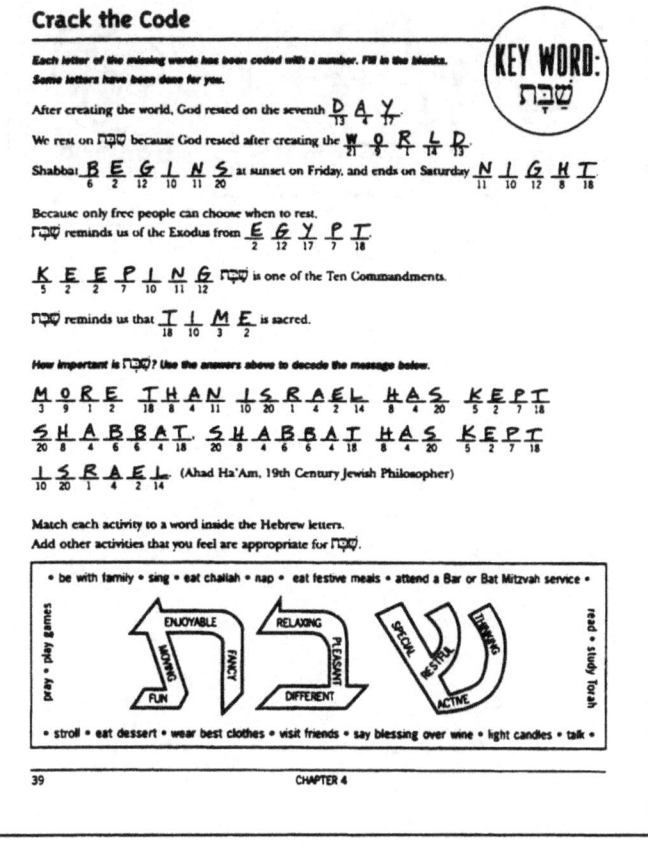

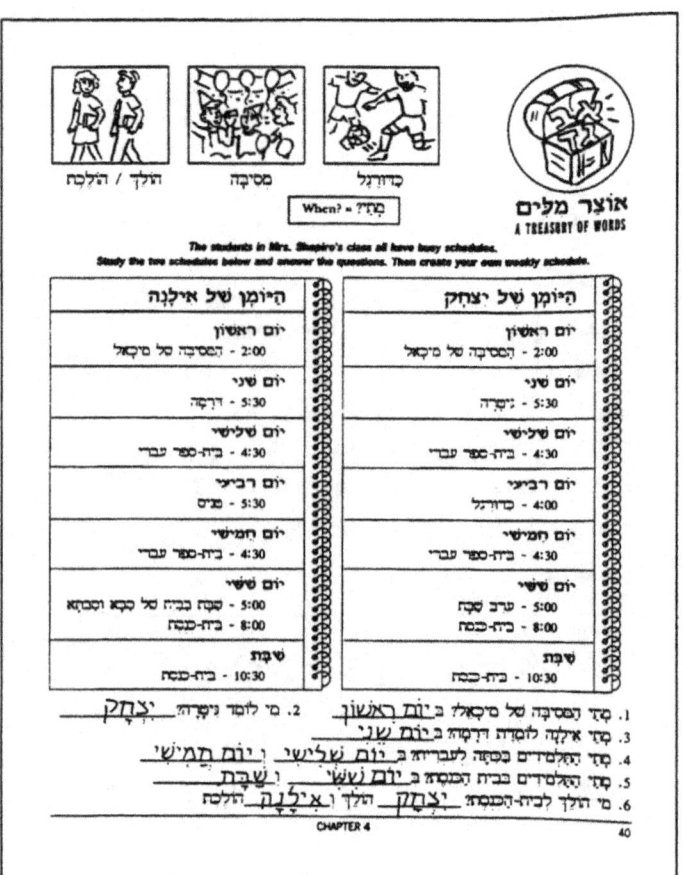

Pages 40-41: Language Enrichment (optional)
הַיּוֹמָן שֶׁלִּי and אוֹצַר מִלִּים

Review the days of the week orally. Call students' attention to the fact that most of the names of the days sound like the corresponding number. For example יוֹם שְׁלִישִׁי the third day, sounds like שָׁלוֹשׁ, or the number three.

Ask students questions in Hebrew about their own schedules. Note that the prefix בְּ precedes any answer that tells what day of the week an event takes place. The word מְסִיבָּה could, technically, be spelled without the י, since the word is vocalized. The word כַּדּוּרֶגֶל can be spelled alternately as two separate words, כַּדּוּר רֶגֶל.

Page 42: Personal Prayer Parchment

Although it is difficult to create the proper milieu for experiencing a שַׁבָּת prayer in the context of a weekday, two methods for doing this are suggested. The first entails the use of guided fantasy. Ask the students to close their eyes and think about a particularly wonderful שַׁבָּת experience they have had. Direct them to concentrate on the warmth of being with their families and friends, the dancing flames of the candles, the joy of singing around the table, and the delicious flavor of the challah, wine, and the festive meal. Alternately, you may choose to create a model שַׁבָּת experience for the students during class time. Assign each student to provide part of the feast. Begin with candles, and go through the entire ritual, including songs and stories. End the session by reciting the prayer while the feelings are still fresh. The method of choice will depend on a number of factors, especially the students' level of שַׁבָּת experience. Students with more limited exposure to שַׁבָּת celebrations will benefit greatly from the more experiential model.

A third possibility for students who have never actually experienced a special שַׁבָּת either at home, at camp, or through Religious School, is to arrange a class שַׁבָּת experience. This could be either a Friday night dinner or שַׁבָּת luncheon after a synagogue service. It's obviously not possible to have an emotional connection to something one has never experienced.

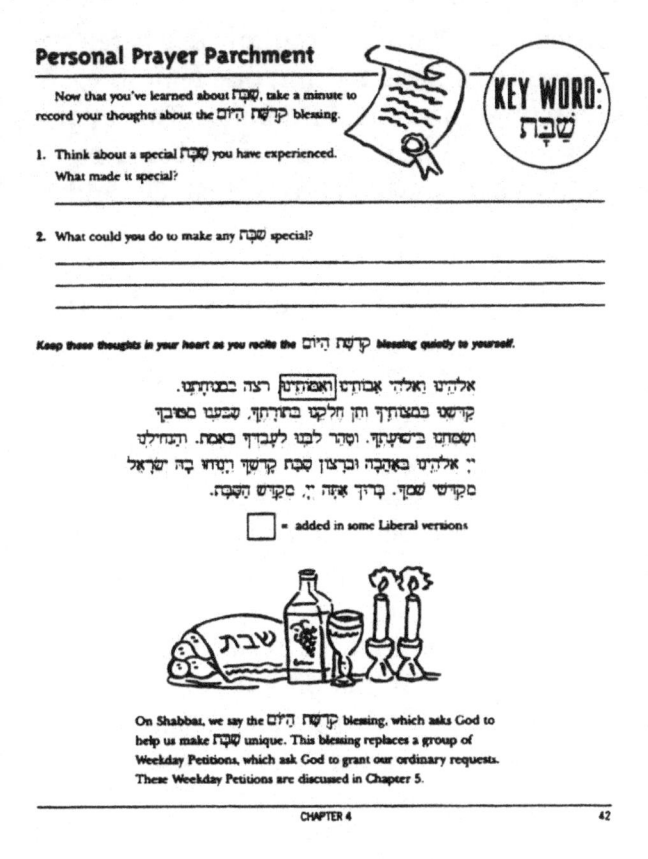

Background Information

In some traditional Siddurim, שַׁבָּת is referred to using three different forms, one feminine, one masculine, and the third plural. This interesting variation in the prayer text is based on the time of day in which it is recited. On Friday evening, the text reads: וְיָנוּחוּ בָהּ יִשְׂרָאֵל מְקַדְּשֵׁי שְׁמֶךָ, using the feminine form בָהּ. During the morning service, the masculine form בוֹ is used: וְיָנוּחוּ בוֹ יִשְׂרָאֵל מְקַדְּשֵׁי שְׁמֶךָ. And during the afternoon service, the plural בָם is used: וְיָנוּחוּ בָם יִשְׂרָאֵל מְקַדְּשֵׁי שְׁמֶךָ. While the Hebrew word שַׁבָּת is generally considered to be a feminine noun, there are instances in the Bible when it is referred to in masculine (such as in Isaiah 56:6).

Tradition provides three explanations for this variation. The first is that on Friday evening, שַׁבָּת is like a bride in her parents' home. Because the joy is derived from her, the feminine form is used. In the morning, שַׁבָּת is like a bride in the groom's home. Because the joy is derived from him, the masculine form is used. By the afternoon, the joy is derived from both, and the plural form is therefore used.

The second explanation links the three forms to three periods of history. Friday evening marks the שַׁבָּת of Creation, a feminine concept expressed through the feminine form בָהּ. Saturday morning marks the שַׁבָּת of Revelation, at which time Israel becomes betrothed to שַׁבָּת. This betrothal is expressed through the masculine form בוֹ. Minchah marks the intimate union between Israel and שַׁבָּת, a union that will eventually lead to the "day that is all שַׁבָּת" (יוֹם שֶׁכֻּלוֹ שַׁבָּת). For this reason, the plural form בָם is used.

The third explanation is mystical in nature, and is derived through Gematria. The numerical value of all three forms, בָהּ + בוֹ + בָם = 57. This has the same numerical value as the word זָן (feed). The implication is that those who rest on שַׁבָּת are sustained by the Almighty.

Our Sages taught: One who delights in שַׁבָּת is given an unbounded heritage, as it is written, "You shall feast on the heritage of your father, Jacob" (Isaiah 58:14).
(*Shabbat* 118a)

Chapter 5 The Weekday Petitions

Core Concept: Our God Hears Our Prayers.

Key Word: prayer תְּפִלָה

Review Vocabulary Words (optional):

one	אֶחָד	You (masc., sing.)	אַתָּה
five	חָמֵשׁ	I	אֲנִי
to, for	לְ_	next to	עַל־יַד
all, every	כָּל	on	עַל
everyone	כָּל אֶחָד	in	בְּ_
every day	כָּל יוֹם	to, for	לְ_
land	אֶרֶץ	of, belonging to	שֶׁל
grandpa	סַבָּא	my	שֶׁלִּי
aunt	דּוֹדָה	to me	לִי
world	עוֹלָם	his	שֶׁלּוֹ
stars	כּוֹכָבִים	hear (masc. sing)	שׁוֹמֵעַ
moon	יָרֵחַ	hear (fem. sing.)	שׁוֹמַעַת
night	לַיְלָה	stand (masc. sing.)	עוֹמֵד
ill people	חוֹלִים	stand (fem. sing.)	עוֹמֶדֶת
ill (masc. sing.)	חוֹלֶה	see (masc. sing.)	רוֹאֶה
healer, doctor	רוֹפֵא		
healer of the ill	רוֹפֵא חוֹלִים		

Polite Words and Greetings

please, you're welcome	בְּבַקָשָׁה	thanks	תּוֹדָה
bon appetit	בְּתֵאָבוֹן	good evening	עֶרֶב טוֹב
happy holiday	חַג שָׂמֵחַ	good morning	בֹּקֶר טוֹב
excuse me	סְלִיחָה		

New Vocabulary Words (optional):

give (masc. sing.)	נוֹתֵן	write (masc. sing.)	כּוֹתֵב
give (fem. sing.)	נוֹתֶנֶת	write (fem. sing.)	כּוֹתֶבֶת
Give! (masc. sing.)	תֵּן	a letter	מִכְתָּב
pray (masc. sing.)	מִתְפַּלֵל	the Western Wall	הַכֹּתֶל הַמַעֲרָבִי
pray (fem. sing.)	מִתְפַּלֶלֶת	a complete healing	רְפוּאָה שְׁלֵמָה

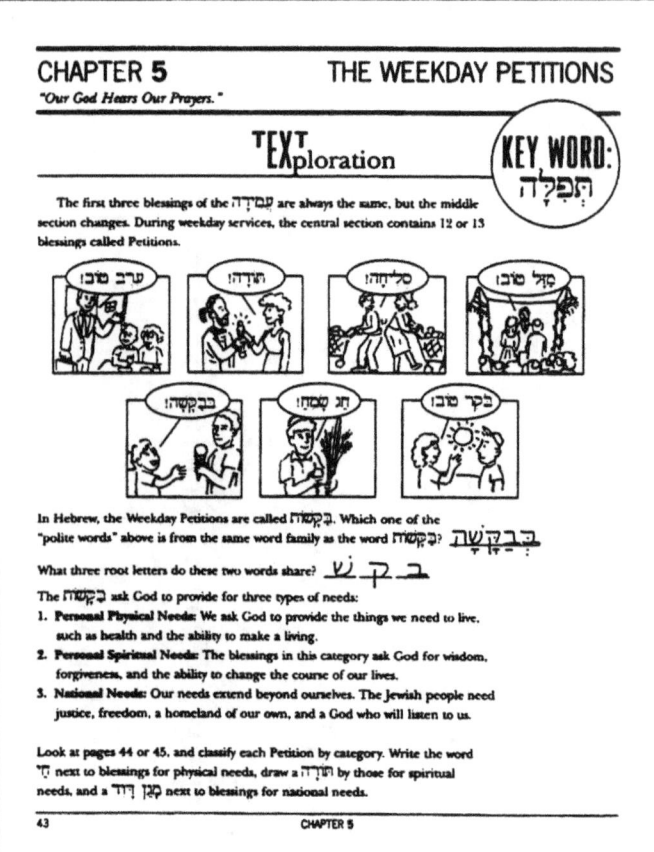

Page 43: Text Exploration

Students should understand that the Petitions are not recited on שַׁבָּת, when they are replaced by the קְדֻשַּׁת הַיּוֹם section. This is because שַׁבָּת is a day to express our appreciation, not for making requests of God. Go over the Hebrew "polite words" with students. Classes that are not completing the Language Enrichment component of the Workbook may be unfamiliar with some of them. All students should complete the entire page. After explaining both activities on this page, students can complete the page independently.

Students may disagree on how to classify each blessing. The "right" answer is much less important than the process of being engaged in examining each blessing to see what it is really asking.

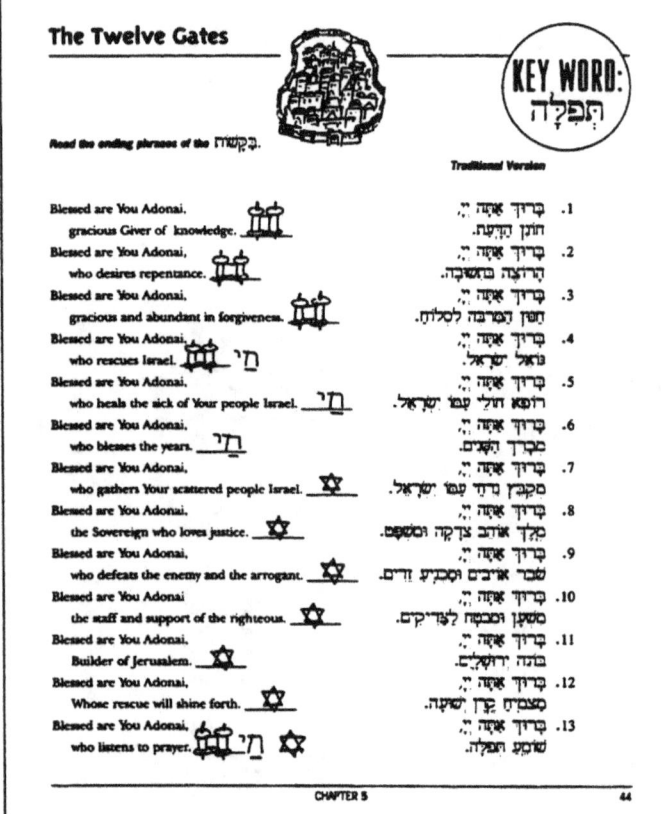

Pages 44-45: The Twelve Gates

The Key Word, תְּפִלָּה, is most often translated as "prayer." However, this English word, derived from an old German root that means "to beg" is utterly inadequate to express the full richness of the Hebrew term. Derived from the root פ.ל.ל., the meanings of which include "to think," "to judge," and "to decide," as well as "to supplicate," and "to entreat," תְּפִלָּה has an essentially introspective quality. True תְּפִלָּה is far more than simply begging favor from a higher authority.

There are many models for conceptualizing Jewish prayer. One can think of it as having a conversation with God in which we express our deepest hopes, or one can think of prayer as having a conversation with ourselves in which we remind ourselves of what is truly important. It is also a way of linking ourselves to other Jews in a binding community, and it affords us the opportunity simply to express our joy and wonder at being alive. As students have now gained a fair amount of experience with prayer, a full discussion of the Key Word תְּפִלָּה can be a springboard for an exploration of all these models.

There are a great many textual variations in the petitionary blessings. While a few of these occur along community lines, even more exist when comparing the Siddur of one denomination with that of another. Even the blessing formulae themselves are not uniform. To add further to the confusion, some Liberal Siddurim include a version of the ninth blessing, while others do not (see Background Information on page 55). These variations are both too numerous and too complex to explore fully within the confines of this short chapter, so only the closing benediction (or חֲתִימָה) of each petition has been included here. If your curriculum includes study of all the weekday petitions, please refer to the text in your congregation's Siddur. Most probably, you will want to use these pages for both reading practice and to illustrate the structure of the עֲמִידָה.

Unless you expect students to be able to read the weekday petitions during worship, do not teach for fluency. Rather, use the pages to provide additional reading practice, both as a phonetic drill and for reading comprehension. Many of the words will be familiar to students, and they may be surprised at how many of the blessings they can actually understand in Hebrew.

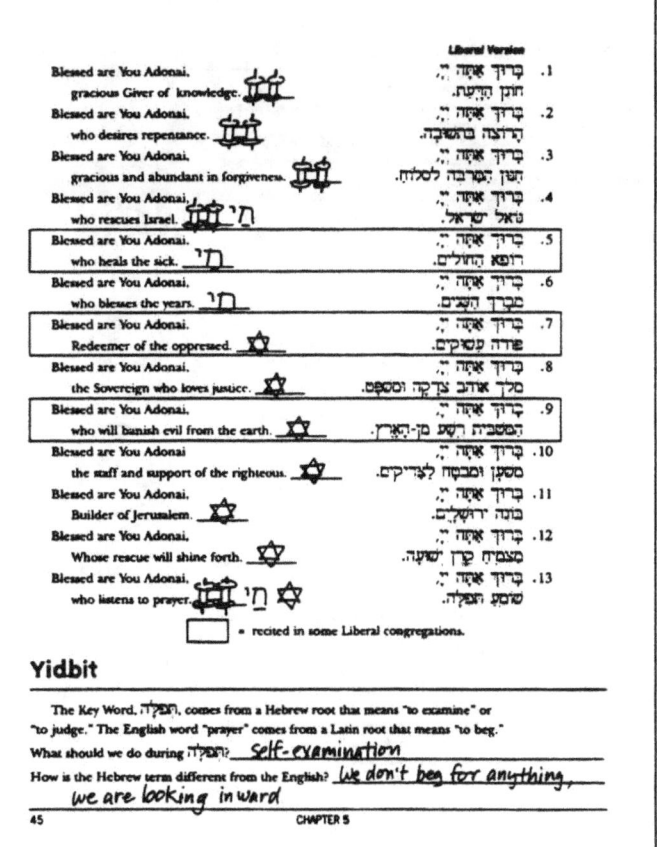

Pages 46-47: That Would Take a Miracle and Judge the Cases

The question of appropriate requests in prayer, which was touched on briefly in Chapter 3, is explored here in depth. Students are introduced to the limits the Rabbis placed on legitimate petitions, and the concept of making a בְּרָכָה לְבַטָּלָה, a vain or wasted prayer. The fictional discussion of Mrs. Shapiro's class on page 46 and the case studies on page 47 provide a sound basis for discussion of this important prayer topic. Read page 46 together with the class. Have students answer the questions on page 47 independently, using their answers as a point of departure for discussion.

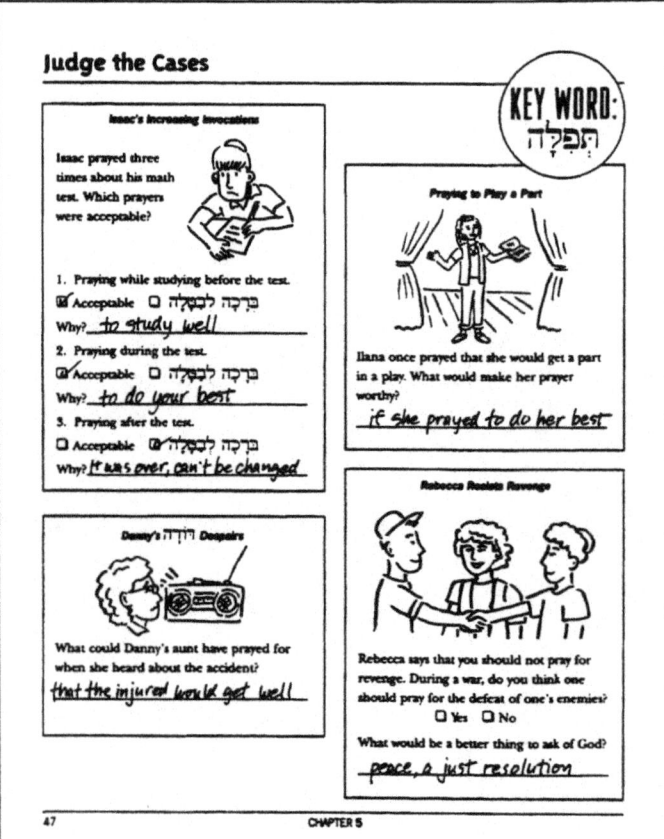

Pages 48-49: Language Enrichment (optional)
אוֹצַר מִלִים

Introduce the new vocabulary orally. Use pictures to illustrate the Western Wall, a letter, and the actions of giving, praying, and writing. Ask questions that let students demonstrate their passive knowledge of the new words, without initially requiring them to use the vocabulary actively. For example,

הַכֹּתֶל הַמַּעֲרָבִי בִּירוּשָׁלַיִם?
הַכֹּתֶל הַמַּעֲרָבִי בְּלוֹנְדוֹן?
הַכֹּתֶל הַמַּעֲרָבִי בְּיִשְׂרָאֵל?

Act out the command form תֵן. Request that students give you objects, using the phrases, "תֵן ___ לְ___" and, "תֵן לִי ___." You can also use pantomime to teach רְפוּאָה שְׁלֵמָה. Student volunteers act ill, saying either, "אֲנִי חוֹלֶה," or, "אֲנִי חוֹלָה." The rest of the class wishes them a "complete recovery." Students can also create their own short skits in pairs.

Page 49 should be completed independently, in class or for homework.

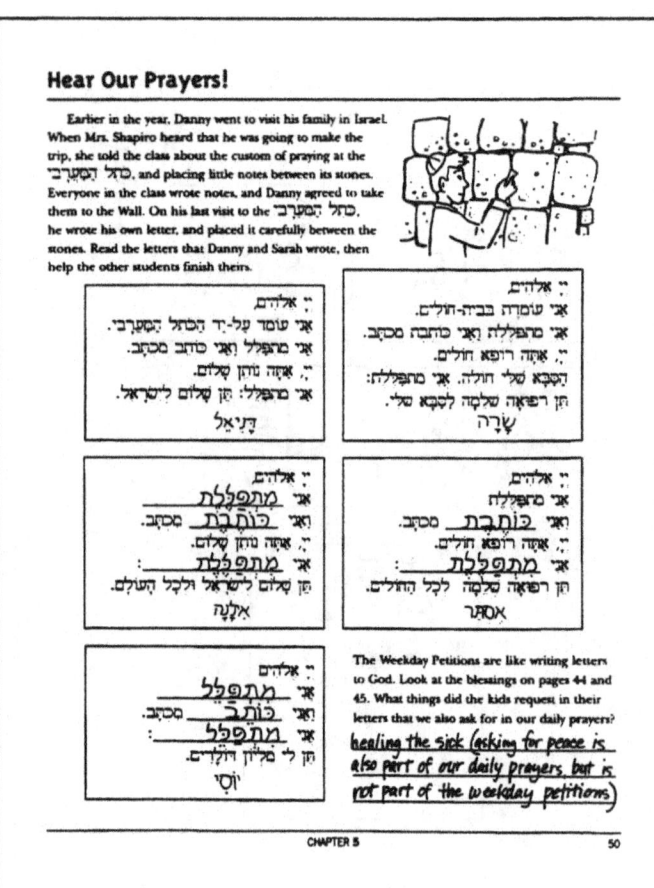

Page 50: Hear Our Prayers!

Read Danny and Sarah's letters aloud with the class. Ask questions in Hebrew to verify that students understand the content. Avoid translating line by line, as this is not advantageous to language learning. Some words are easier to explain without using translation. If students are confused by the word עוֹמֵד, you can easily stand up and say, "אֲנִי עוֹמֵד" or "אֲנִי עוֹמֶדֶת". Use translation only if a phrase defies your attempts to explain it any other way. However, it is better to translate than to leave students frustrated.

Go over the unfinished letters as well, making sure students understand the content and what they should fill in. Have them complete the page independently so they receive an additional exposure to reading.

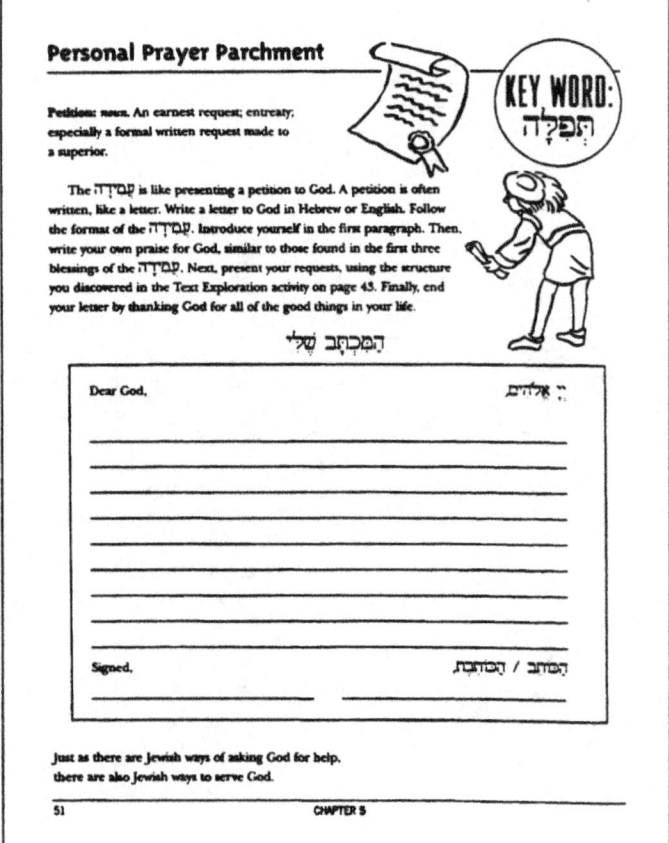

Page 51: Personal Prayer Parchment

One of the themes repeated in this chapter is the notion of writing one's personal prayer, and placing it in the הַכֹּתֶל הַמַּעֲרָבִי. According to one legend, all of our sincere prayers are carried from wherever we are and gather at that holy site before ascending to God.

Show the class a picture of people praying at the הַכֹּתֶל הַמַּעֲרָבִי, and ask them to hold the image of this place in their minds. Then direct them to close their eyes, pray with all their hearts for something that is important to them, and imagine that their prayers are flying there.

Background Information

Of all the weekday petitionary blessings, the most controversial is also the newest. According to *Berachot* 28b, this benediction was added by the order of Rabban Gamaliel after the destruction of the Temple in the first century C.E., and was composed by Samuel the Lesser. The original blessing was worded in such a way that members of the various sects, especially the newly emerging Christians, would be unable to lead communal worship. Over the centuries, this blessing was edited by various Jewish and Christian censors to the point that its original phrasing is impossible to determine. The Middle Ages brought a new threat to the Jewish community's precarious existence in Europe, as some Jewish converts to Christianity began to slander their former coreligionists in order to gain greater clout within their new religious circle.

In the nineteenth century, as European states began to grant citizenship to their Jewish inhabitants, the Reform movement emerged with its philosophy of seeking a balance between Judaism and the pull of modernity. The early Reform Rabbis felt that this blessing was unnecessary (as citizenship removed the threat of apostate slanderers), and also ran contrary to the spirit of humanism that underlies modernity. As a result, the most traditional versions of their petitionary blessings eliminated this benediction, and contained a total of 18 blessings in the weekday עֲמִידָה. In recent years, Reform Siddurim have begun to include a new version of this blessing, which expresses the desire to rid the world of all evil rulers, and to establish a world in which the lives of all people will be ennobled.

Chapter 6 עֲבוֹדָה

Core Concept: Ask Not What God Can Do for You; Ask What You Can Do for God.

Key Word: work, service עֲבוֹדָה

Review Vocabulary Words (optional):

synagogue	בֵּית־כְּנֶסֶת	doctor (fem.)	רוֹפְאָה
school	בֵּית־סֵפֶר	she	הִיא
books	סְפָרִים	he	הוּא
library	סִפְרִיָה	who?	מִי
librarian (fem.)	סַפְרָנִית	where?	אֵיפֹה
Talmud	תַּלְמוּד	give (fem. sing.)	נוֹתֶנֶת
Hebrew	עִבְרִית	write (masc. sing.)	כּוֹתֵב
history	הִיסְטוֹרִיָה	go, walk (masc. sing.)	הוֹלֵךְ
hospital	בֵּית־חוֹלִים	see (masc. sing.)	רוֹאֶה
ill people	חוֹלִים	all, every	כָּל
doctor (masc.)	רוֹפֵא	everyone	כָּל אֶחָד

New Vocabulary Words (optional):

work (masc. sing.)	עוֹבֵד
work (fem. sing.)	עוֹבֶדֶת
teach (masc. sing.)	מְלַמֵד
teach (fem. sing.)	מְלַמֶדֶת
sermon	דְבַר תּוֹרָה

Page 52: Ask Not What God Can Do for You; Ask What You Can Do for God.

The idea of service in all its varying forms is the central unifying element of this chapter. Here the relationship between the ancient sacrificial service, the worship service that replaced it, and the performing of community service are examined. The Key Word עֲבוֹדָה actually encompasses all three of these meanings.

The Key Word עֲבוֹדָה has two related meanings, "work" (as in עָבַד אֶת הָאֲדָמָה — work or till the soil) and "worship" (עָבַד אֶת הָאֱלֹהִים — serve or worship God). To the biblical mind, the relationship between God and worshipers was that of master and servant. It is interesting to note that the biblical concept of "slavery" when applied to Jewish slaves as opposed to Canaanite slaves, was actually a form of indentured servitude. At the Sabbatical year, all עֲבָדִים were freed.

At its core, the root ע.ב.ד. means "service." Thus, one's profession is a way of providing a service to others, just as one's worship is performing a service for God. The root word activity on page 52 allows students to explore the connection between the two basic meanings of the root word ע.ב.ד.

This page asks students to locate forms of the Key Word in the prayer text, and isolate the three root letters. This type of activity is beneficial for both decoding fluency and reading comprehension. Students are required to read and locate phrases drawn from the text. This increased exposure to the text aids in reading fluency. By having students identify words from the same root, they are able to increase their comprehension of the general themes and concepts that appear in the prayer. Students are not expected to be able to translate a text, but rather to identify what the topic might be, based on their knowledge of selected root words and vocabulary.

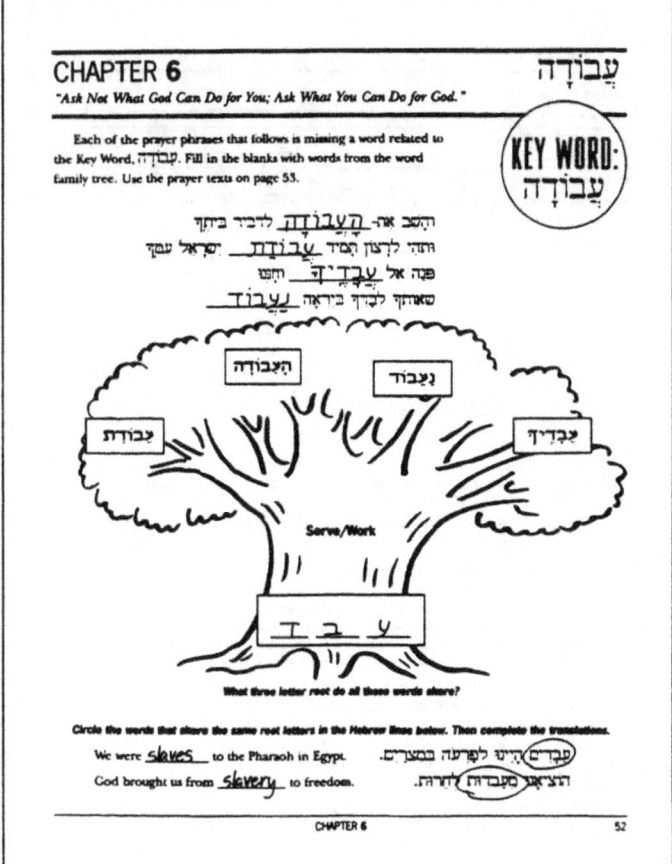

Page 53: The Twelve Gates and Understanding the Prayer Differences

The central differences between the Traditional and Liberal versions of this prayer involve the question of whether or not it is desirable to rebuild the Temple in Jerusalem and return to the practice of offering animal sacrifices. While this has been a moot question for two millenia, the issue is beginning to surface in Israel today.

Opinions concerning this controversial issue are not uniform by denomination, although the vast majority of Reform, Conservative, and Reconstructionist Jews are opposed to a return to such practices. Among Orthodox scholars, opinions range acroìss the spectrum. Maimonides declared that animal sacrifices were nothing more than a stepping stone in the development of Jewish worship, a way of approaching worship of the One God that was familiar and comfortable to people in ancient times. Yet, he maintained that prayer, study, and performing mitzvot are higher forms of service.

As with other controversial topics raised by the liturgy, students are asked to confront this issue directly in the Understanding the Prayer Differences section at the bottom of page 53.

Page 54: Serving God with Your Heart and Your Hands

The connection between serving God and serving others is developed in the story and activity on this page. Be sure students do not interpret the Prophet's quotes to mean that prayer is not a valid way of serving God. Rather, the point is that prayer and fasting alone are not enough. God also requires that we serve our communities by aiding those in need.

Read the story and the quotations together with the class. Then have students complete the questions independently in class or for homework. You can discuss the questions either before or after students complete the assignment.

Pages 55-56: Language Enrichment (optional)
אוֹצָר מִלִּים

The language activity is linked to both the chapter's Key Word and Core Concept. עֲבוֹדָה is not only the word for a worship service, it is also the modern Hebrew word for work or service. In the examples given here, each of the adults is working in a service profession. Teach the new vocabulary orally first, using pictures or props to illustrate the professions. Choose student volunteers to play the role of each worker. Props can be very simple: a tongue depressor for the doctor, chalk and a history book for a teacher, etc. As you hand out props, review the names of the professions, asking questions in Hebrew about who wants to play which part. Then introduce the new verbs עוֹבֵד and עוֹבֶדֶת. Draw pictures on the board of the places where each person works: the hospital, school, synagogue, and library. Now, use the new verb to ask questions that other students can answer with simple one word answers. This technique lets students passively understand the new verb before you require them to use it actively. A sample question might be, "מִי עוֹבֵד בְּבֵית חוֹלִים?" Students could answer with either the name of the student playing the role, or with the words "רוֹפֵא" or "רוֹפְאָה." More advanced students can be encouraged to use complete sentences. Teach the new verb מְלַמֶּדֶת/מְלַמֵּד by using a variety of teacher props and asking what subject each teacher teaches. Props could include a tennis racket, different books (including Hebrew), or a guitar. After making statements like, "הִיא מְלַמֶּדֶת עִבְרִית," ask questions such as, "מָה אַתְּ מְלַמֶּדֶת?"

After this oral introduction, read both pages with students. Students can then complete the pages independently.

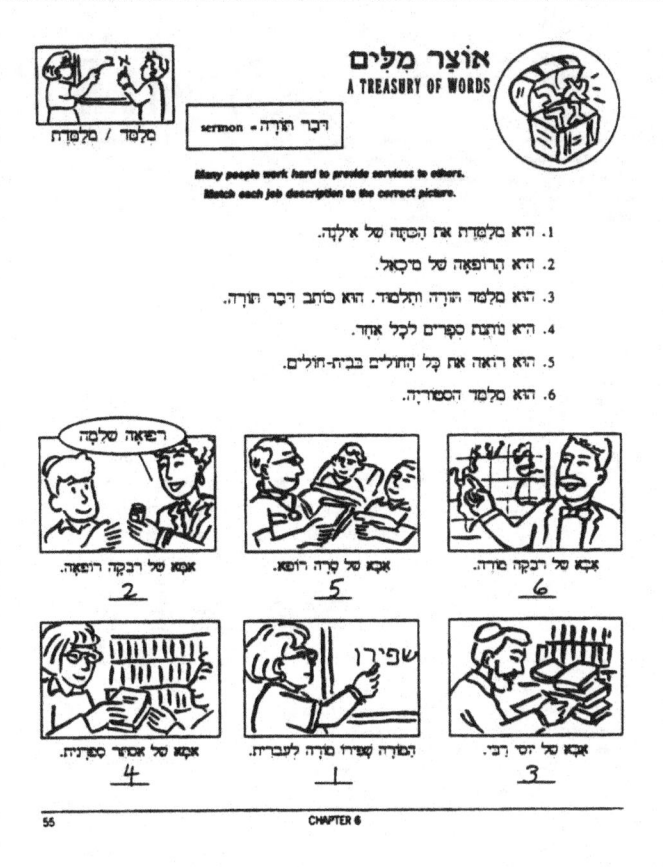

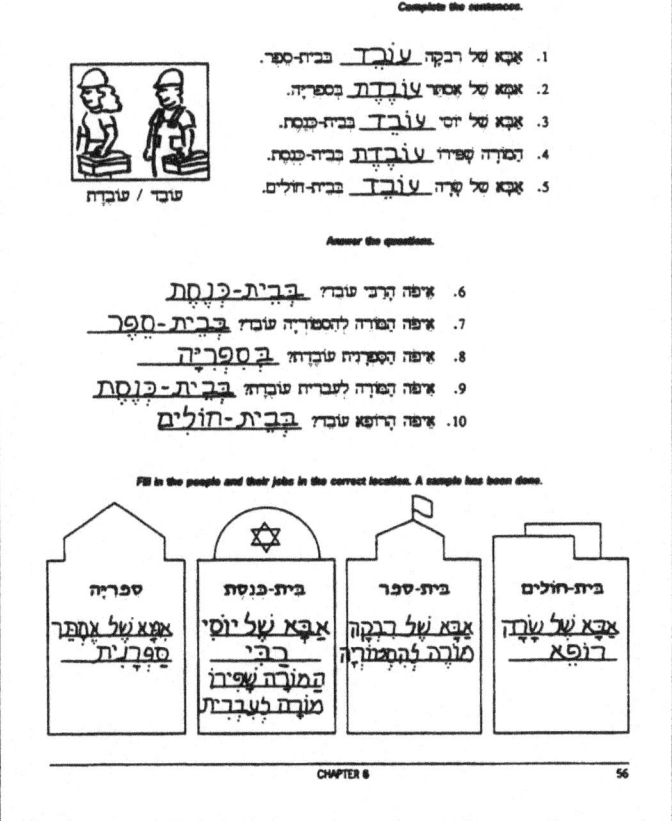

Page 57: Personal Prayer Parchment

Do a short classroom service project for the congregation or community. This could be as simple as cleaning up around the synagogue's grounds, making Shabbat or holiday greeting cards for residents of a local nursing home, or asking students to bring in food or clothing for the poor in the community. Immediately after completing this project, recite the עֲבוֹדָה as a class, and discuss the relationship between serving others and serving God.

Background Information

The עֲבוֹדָה marks the beginning of the final section of the עֲמִידָה, as its final three blessings are categorized as blessings of thanksgiving. According to Millgram (p. 102), these three benedictions share a common origin in the service of the Temple in Jerusalem. As such, the עֲבוֹדָה is one of the oldest paragraphs in the עֲמִידָה. A version of it was recited daily in the Temple as the priests completed the morning sacrifices. With the destruction of the Temple, the Rabbis declared that reciting this prayer at the time when sacrifices would normally have been offered was an acceptable substitute for actually offering sacrifices. The loss of the Temple Service necessitated some changes within the text of the עֲבוֹדָה.

According to Macy Nulman (p. 274), two phrases in the prayer imply that the Temple's destruction has already taken place, and thus would not have been part of the original version. These are:
וְהָשֵׁב אֶת־הָעֲבוֹדָה לִדְבִיר בֵּיתֶךָ
(and restore the service of Your sanctuary)
and וְתֶחֱזֶינָה עֵינֵינוּ בְּשׁוּבְךָ לְצִיּוֹן בְּרַחֲמִים
(May we see Your return to Zion in mercy)
He further states that the original closing benediction was: שֶׁאוֹתְךָ לְבַדְּךָ בְּיִרְאָה נַעֲבוֹד,
(Whom alone we serve in awe), as used in some Liberal versions of the text.

Chapter 7 הוֹדָאָה

Core Concept: Our God Deserves Our Thanks.

Key Word: thank you תּוֹדָה

Review Vocabulary Words (optional):

fish	דָג	in the __	בַּ__
fruit salad	סָלַט פֵּרוֹת	all, every	כֹּל
moon	יָרֵחַ	love (masc. sing.)	אוֹהֵב
sun	שֶׁמֶשׁ	love (fem. sing.)	אוֹהֶבֶת
bird	צִפּוֹר	write (masc. sing.)	כּוֹתֵב
name	שֵׁם	letter	מִכְתָּב
language	שָׂפָה	see (fem. sing.)	רוֹאָה
brother	אָח	I	אֲנִי
brothers	אַחִים	you (fem. sing.)	אַתְּ
Sunday	יוֹם רִאשׁוֹן	he	הוּא
coffee house, cafe	בֵּית קָפֶה	she	הִיא
good appetite, bon appetit!	בְּתֵאָבוֹן	__ has	יֵשׁ לְ__
with	עִם	of, belonging to	שֶׁל
without	בְּלִי	his	שֶׁלוֹ
under	תַּחַת		

New Vocabulary Words (optional):

egg	בֵּיצָה	want (masc. sing.)	רוֹצֶה
milk	חָלָב	want (fem. sing)	רוֹצָה
dinner	אֲרוּחַת עֶרֶב	also	גַּם
lunch	אֲרוּחַת צָהֳרַיִם	thank you very much	תּוֹדָה רַבָּה
breakfast	אֲרוּחַת בֹּקֶר		

New Language Elements

The first plural pronoun: we אֲנַחְנוּ

The remaining plural pronouns will be presented in Chapter 8.

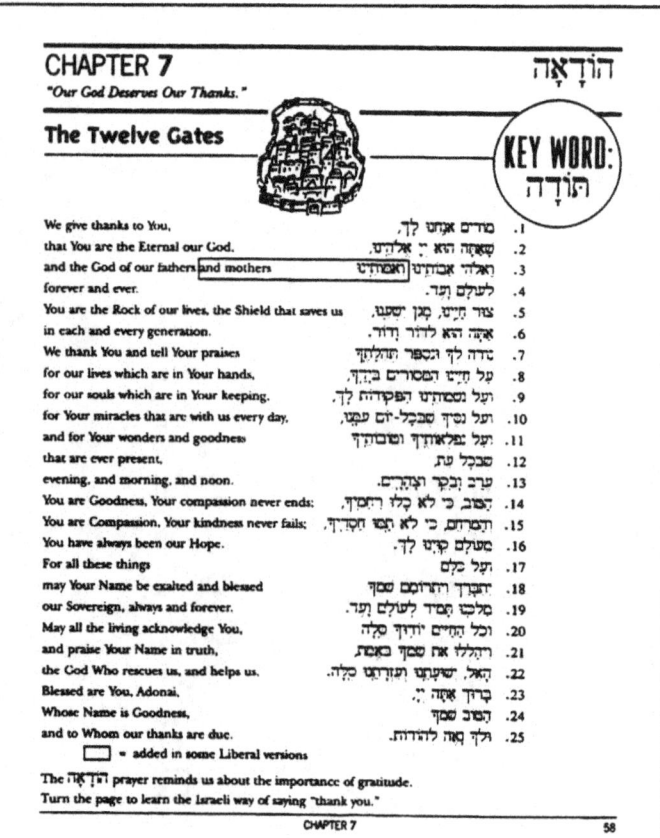

Page 58: The Twelve Gates

Only one difference exists between the Traditional and Liberal versions of the הוֹדָאָה, namely the addition of the אִמָּהוֹת in the Liberal version. If students are unclear about the reasons for this addition, they can review the material on page 11, where the concept was introduced.

If students will not be required to recite this prayer aloud in a worship service, you may choose to teach them to read it correctly, but not spend a great deal of time drilling for reading fluency.

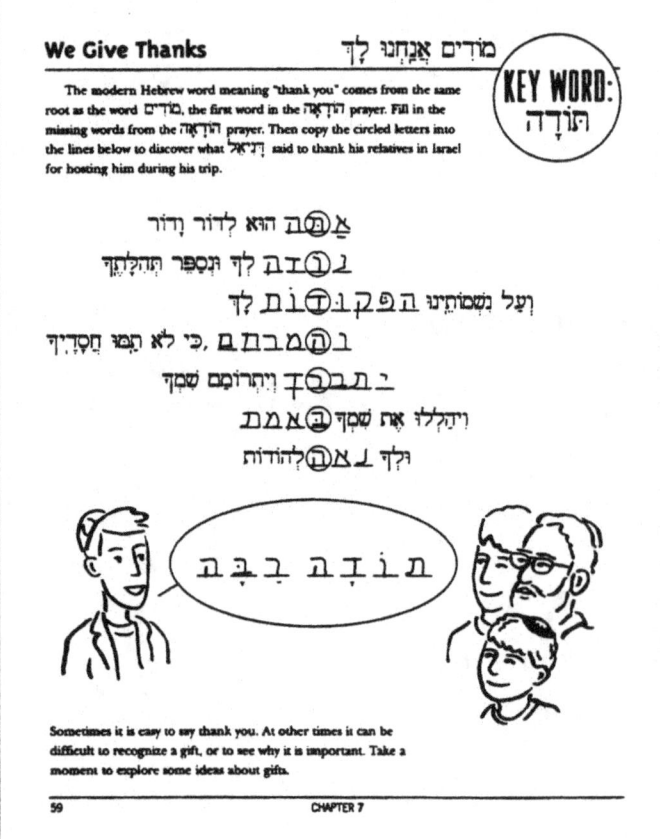

Page 59: We Give Thanks
מוֹדִים אֲנַחְנוּ לָךְ

This page provides additional reading practice using phrases from the prayer. It can be done independently in class, or for homework. The activity makes the connection between the prayer text, the prayer concept of thanking God, and the modern Hebrew words for thank you, תּוֹדָה רַבָּה.

Of all the Key Words that students have studied in the course of this program, תּוֹדָה is straightforward and easy to grasp, as the English phrase "thank you" successfully conveys it in all contexts. It is also an eminently useful little word to know. The activity on page 59 provides the opportunity for students to connect the Key Word and its modern usage with the opening words of the prayer. The Yidbit on page 64 affords the chance to review a basic concept from Book 1 of this series, (i.e., the notion that reciting prayers and בְּרָכוֹת is the Jewish way of expressing our thanks to God for all the wonders of this world that we might otherwise take for granted).

**Page 60: For All These Things
We Give You Thanks**

The most basic concept presented in the הוֹדָאָה prayer is that God, as the source of all blessing, is deserving of our thanks. Related to the notion of giving thanks is the question of whether or not God answers our prayers by giving us the "gifts" we request. This issue is raised in the Mrs. Shapiro story, and is discussed around the issue of saying thank you for gifts that we don't really want. This issue will most probably spark student interest, with students vying to tell of the worst gifts they have received. Be sure to bring the discussion back to the theological concept! We need to be thankful to God for the gifts we receive on a daily basis, gifts that we often take for granted.

Most of us think of miracles as extraordinary events that defy the laws of nature. The Rabbis, however, point to a different kind of miracle — those so common that we take them for granted, and fail to realize how miraculous they are. These gifts, such as our health, or an environment that sustains our lives, are truly gifts that are necessary for our existence. Thus, while we might consider our prayers unanswered if we pray for achievements or outcomes that elude us, in actuality all of us can be thankful for the blessings we constantly receive.

Page 61: Language Enrichment (optional)
אוֹצַר מִלִּים

In זְמַן לִתְפִילָה Book 2: שְׁמַע, students were introduced to the singular pronouns, and were given many opportunities to practice them. Here the first plural pronoun, אֲנַחְנוּ, is introduced, and is drilled using simple declarative sentences. These sentences also review vocabulary introduced earlier in this Workbook, or in Book 2. The remaining plural pronouns will be introduced in the next chapter.

Before having students complete the page independently, introduce the new pronoun orally. First, demonstrate its meaning by using simple sentences to describe you and your students. Point to yourself and say,
"אֲנִי מוֹרָה. אֲנִי בַּכִּתָּה."
Then, point to a boy and say,
"הוּא יֶלֶד. הוּא בַּכִּתָּה."
Then, making a hand motion that includes both you and the student, say, "אֲנַחְנוּ בַּכִּתָּה." If, after doing this several times, students seem unclear, translate the pronoun once. Next, have students divide themselves into groups of two or three students. Each group will pantomine a situation similar to those depicted in the Workbook and then offer three descriptions in Hebrew of what they are doing, using the new pronoun אֲנַחְנוּ. The rest of the class needs to choose which sentence describes what the group is doing. Since students have not yet learned the other plural pronouns, they won't be able to answer by using Hebrew sentences to say, "You are . . . " You can have them repeat back only part of the sentence, eliminating the pronoun, use the students' names, or have them indicate which answer they think is correct by raising their hands.

Page 62-63: Language Enrichment (optional)
אוֹצַר מִלִּים

אֲרוּחַת בֹּקֶר וְגַם אֲרוּחַת צָהֳרַיִם

The names of the meals אֲרוּחַת עֶרֶב and (אֲרוּחַת בֹּקֶר, אֲרוּחַת צָהֳרַיִם) are taught, since the Hebrew words for morning, noon, and evening (בֹּקֶר, צָהֳרַיִם, עֶרֶב) appear in the prayer text.

Teach the new vocabulary using pictures, toy food, or the actual food. Assemble sample meals, and ask students to identify the names of the foods and the meals. Act out the conversation, either in groups of five, or with one group performing in front of the class. The fifth student will play the role of the waiter or waitress. This can be a silent role for a weaker student, or a stronger student could be encouraged to improvise the part. After acting out the conversation as it is written" in the Workbook, have students create their own versions of the situation. These can be very similar in plot to the story in the Workbook, or they can use their own creativity. You can also have students create their own Hebrew menus. They can do this as a homework assignment, and cut out magazine pictures to illustrate the menus.

The word שְׁתִיָּה, meaning beverage, appears on the menu, but is not used in the language activity, nor does it appear elsewhere in the Workbook. Students should be able to understand its meaning in context, and may use it if they create their own menus, but otherwise do not need to learn it.

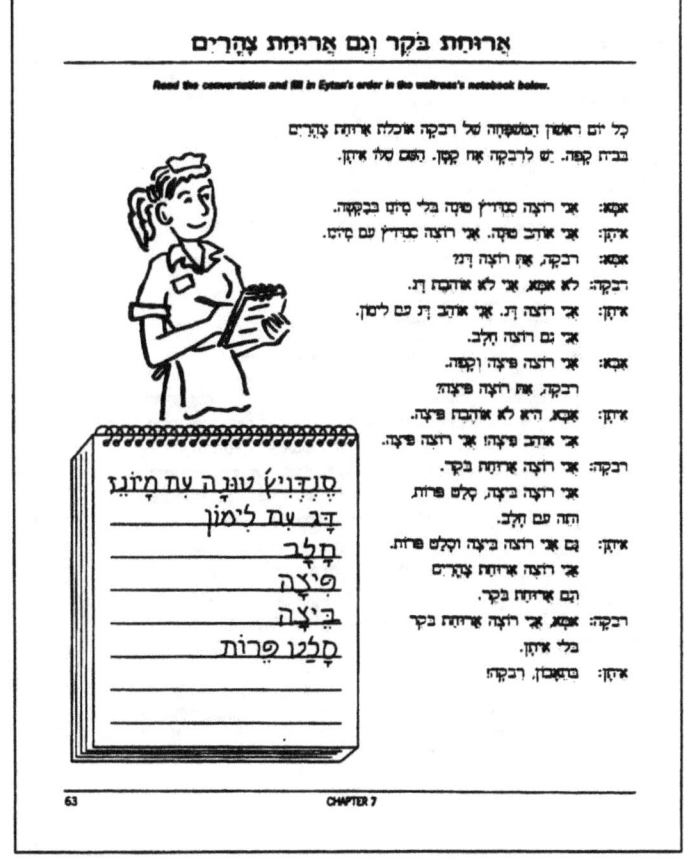

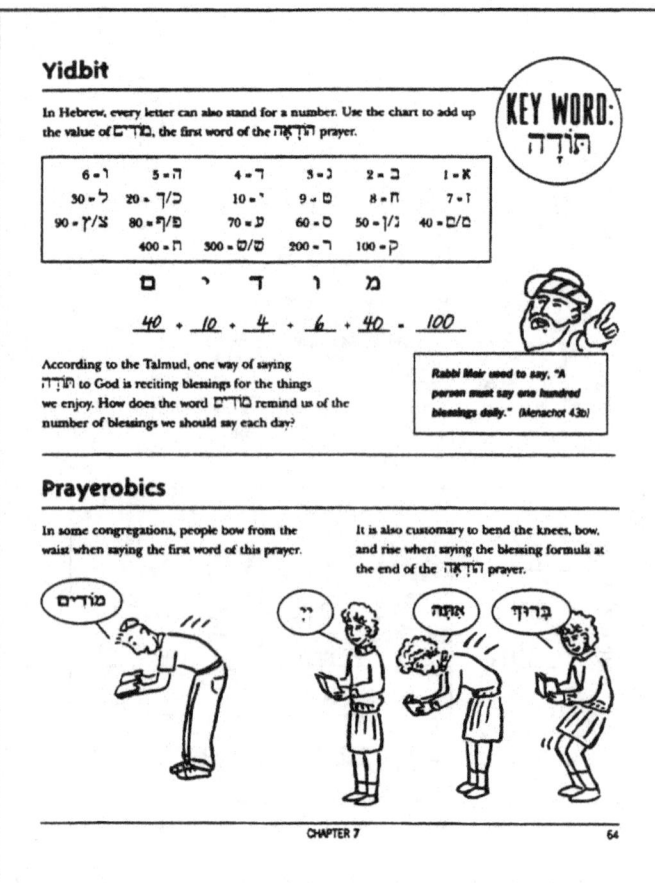

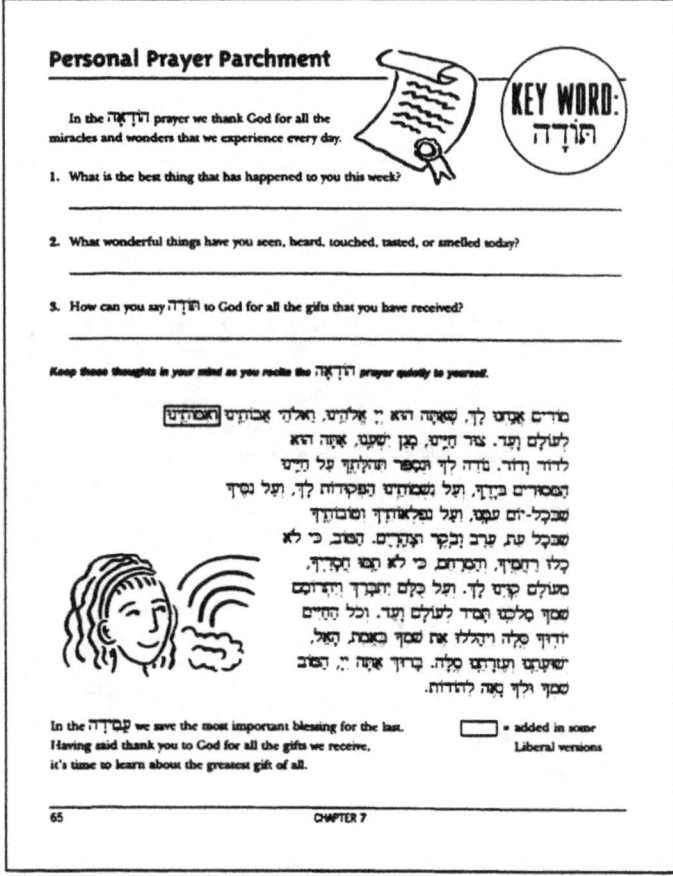

Page 64: Yidbit and Prayerobics

Have students independently figure out the numerological value of the word מוֹדִים. This opening word of the הוֹדָאָה has the numerical value of one hundred (מ = 40, י = 10, ד = 4, and ו = 6). This is linked to Rabbi Meir's declaration that as a proper expression of gratitude to God, a person should recite one hundred brachot each day (*Menachot* 43b).

Next, go over the Yidbit with the whole class, reviewing the concept of Hebrew letters having a number value. Explain that letters are commonly used in Israel for the days of the week and for classes in school. Sunday is יוֹם א׳; second grade is כִּתָּה ב׳. Even more important, chapters and verses in the Bible are cited in Hebrew using letters to represent numbers. If this is part of your Judaica curriculum, take the opportunity now to have students use the number chart to help them locate biblical verses.

Teach students the Prayerobics movements if they are used in your congregation. If they are not used, encourage students to try them during your class worship service.

Page 65: Personal Prayer Parchment

Brainstorm a list of "everyday miracles." Write each item from the list on a small slip of paper, and place the slips in a paper bag. In small groups or individually, ask students to select one slip from the bag, and then design thank-you cards, similar to commercial greeting cards, which thank God for the selected miracle.

Post the designs on a bulletin board with an enlarged version of the הוֹדָאָה text in the center.

Background Information

Like both the preceding prayer and the morning version of the prayer that follows it, the הוֹדָאָה was originally part of the ancient Temple service. When the Temple was destroyed in 70 C.E., the הוֹדָאָה was inserted into the עֲמִידָה. At that point, a number of rules were developed for its recitation. For example, the Talmud (*Berachot* 33b, *Megillah* 25a) proscribes repeating the opening word of the blessing, (i.e., מוֹדִים, מוֹדִים), as it might appear that one is appealing to two powers, rather than a single God. Further, according to Nulman (p. 252), the early Christians began their blessings over wine, bread, and food by saying מוֹדִים, מוֹדִים.

In congregations that repeat the עֲמִידָה, there are special rules for the *Shaliach Tzibur* to follow for reciting the הוֹדָאָה. While the other blessings may be repeated quietly and quickly, the *Shaliach Tzibur* is required to chant the הוֹדָאָה aloud, so that at least ten people can hear it. This highlights the centrality of the הוֹדָאָה, as its communal repetition was instituted to allow those who are not capable of reciting it to fulfill the obligation of thanking God.

In Talmudic times, an abbreviated version of the הוֹדָאָה was developed. Known as Modim DeRabbanan (Thanksgiving of the Rabbis), it comprises the individual prayers that various sages recited during the repetition of the הוֹדָאָה.

While the Precentor recites the paragraph "We give thanks," what does the congregation say? Rab declared: "We give thanks unto You, O Eternal our God, because we are able to give You thanks." Samuel declared: "God of all flesh, seeing that we give You thanks." Rabbi Simlai bar Abba declared: "Our Creator and Creator of all things in the beginning, seeing that we give You thanks." The men of Nehardea declared in the name of Rabbi Simlai: "Blessings and thanksgiving to Your great Name because You have kept us alive and preserved us, seeing that we give You thanks." Rabbi Aha bar Ya'akov used to conclude thus: "So may You continue to keep us alive and be gracious to us; and gather us together and assemble our exiles to Your holy courts to observe Your statutes and to do Your will with a perfect heart, seeing that we give You thanks." Rabbi Papa said: "Consequently let us recite them all." (*Sotah* 40a)

While a worshiper may simply add "Amen" at the end of the other blessings to fulfill the obligation of reciting them, giving thanks is so personal that it cannot adequately be done through an intermediary. Each person is responsible for saying his or her own thank-you.

A number of special texts are added to the הוֹדָאָה for holidays. On Chanukah and Purim, the prayer עַל הַנִּסִּים is added. In traditional Siddurim, this passage is inserted before the final blessing of the הוֹדָאָה. It is inserted between the הוֹדָאָה and the benediction for שָׁלוֹם in some Liberal Siddurim. Other insertions are made during the High Holy Days.

Chapter 8 שָׁלוֹם רָב

Core Concept: Our God Is the God of Peace.

Key Word: peace, hello, good-bye שָׁלוֹם

Review Vocabulary Words (optional):

learn (masc. sing.)	לוֹמֵד	next to	עַל-יַד
see (fem. sing.)	רוֹאָה	mother (formal)	אֵם
eat (masc. sing.)	אוֹכֵל	father (formal)	אָב
hear (fem. sing.)	שׁוֹמַעַת	king, ruler	מֶלֶךְ
walk, go (masc. sing.)	הוֹלֵךְ	doctor (masc.)	רוֹפֵא
walk, go (fem. sing.)	הוֹלֶכֶת	doctor (fem.)	רוֹפְאָה
love (fem. sing.)	אוֹהֶבֶת	ill (masc. sing.)	חוֹלֶה
she	הִיא	ill (fem. sing.)	חוֹלָה
we	אֲנַחְנוּ	good (masc.)	טוֹב
her	שֶׁלָּה	good morning	בֹּקֶר טוֹב
his	שֶׁלּוֹ	good evening	עֶרֶב טוֹב
who	מִי	dinner	אֲרוּחַת עֶרֶב

New Vocabulary Words (optional):

How are you? (said to a male)	מַה שְׁלוֹמְךָ?
How are you? (said to a female)	מַה שְׁלוֹמֵךְ?
you (masc. pl.)	אַתֶּם
you (fem. pl.)	אַתֶּן
they (masc.)	הֵם
they (fem.)	הֵן

Plural Pronouns

The direct object marker אֶת is presented but not analyzed.

Page 66: Reading Page

This page can be used to provide reading practice, or to introduce a discussion on the subject of peace, the theme of this chapter's prayer. Use the song "A Song For Peace" as a springboard for talking about how Israelis desire peace, and in particular, Yitzhak Rabin's desire for peace. The song says that we must demand peace "with a great shout," since those that have died in battle can never be "brought back to here."

An actual literary analysis of the prayer may be counterproductive, as its message on close inspection appears anti-religious. The song says that neither "the purest of prayers" nor "Songs of Praise (שִׁירֵי הַלֵּל)" will restore the dead to life. It advises, "Don't whisper a prayer . . . just sing a song for peace." While it might be argued that the message of the song is that an active response is needed to bring peace, prayer is used as a symbol of passive acceptance. Why then include the song in a prayer program? Simply because its association with the assassination of Rabin has given the song itself symbolic meaning far beyond its actual words. Here is the story of a Jewish leader who lost his life because of his quest for peace, who died after singing a song of peace, with the blood splattered words of the song found on his body.

A recording of the song is on the *Israel 50th Anniversary Album*, available from Tara Publications.

Page 67: שָׁלוֹם רָב

In an effort to acknowledge that God is the universal Sovereign of all humanity, some Liberal versions of this prayer add the phrase וְאֶת־כָּל־הָעַמִּים (and all peoples) to the line:

וְטוֹב בְּעֵינֶיךָ לְבָרֵךְ אֶת־עַמְּךָ יִשְׂרָאֵל
בְּכָל־עֵת וּבְכָל־שָׁעָה בִּשְׁלוֹמֶךָ

which requests that God bless Israel with peace. The reasoning behind this addition is discussed in the Understanding the Prayer Differences section of Chapter 9 on page 74 of the Workbook, since the שִׂים שָׁלוֹם prayer contains the same addition.

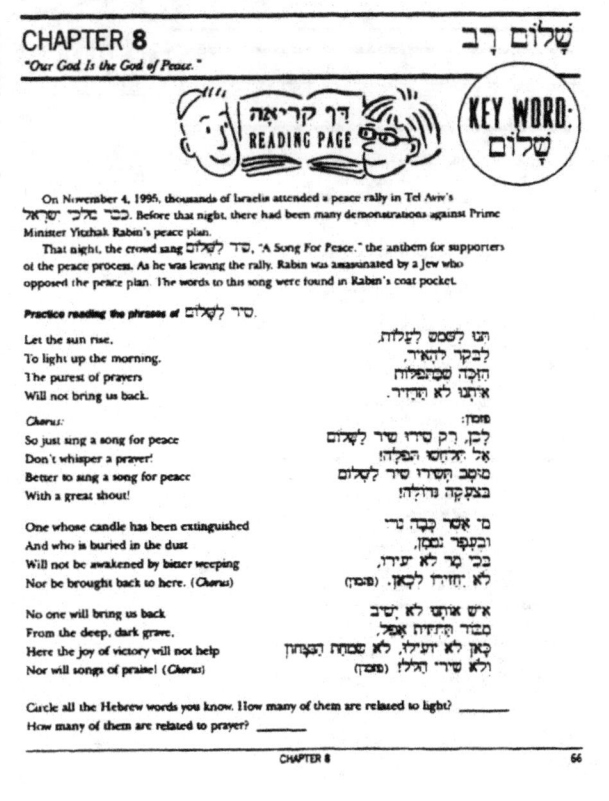

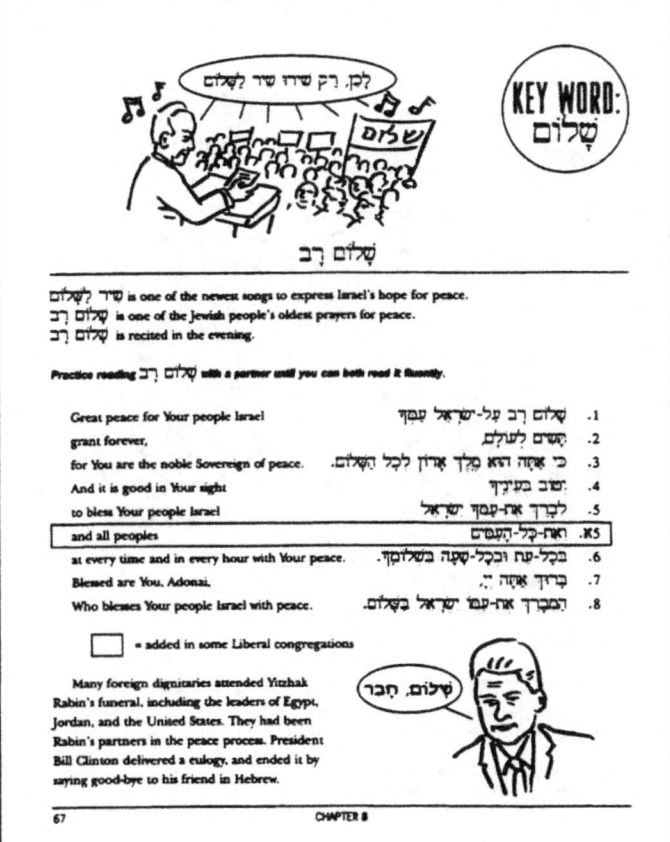

Page 68: שָׁלוֹם, חָבֵר

God as the Source of peace is the central theme of this chapter. Connected to this theme is the peace process between Israel and her Arab neighbors, and the tragic loss of Yitzhak Rabin. The Mrs. Shapiro class story on page 68 deals directly with these connections, and the prayer text on page 67 is bookended by "A Song For Peace" and President Clinton's famous farewell, שָׁלוֹם, חָבֵר, which he said in his eulogy at Rabin's funeral.

Read the story together with the class. To expand the discussion, you can bring in photographs of Israel for a bulletin board, books or magazine articles about Israel, or invite a speaker to class who has either lived in or visited Israel.

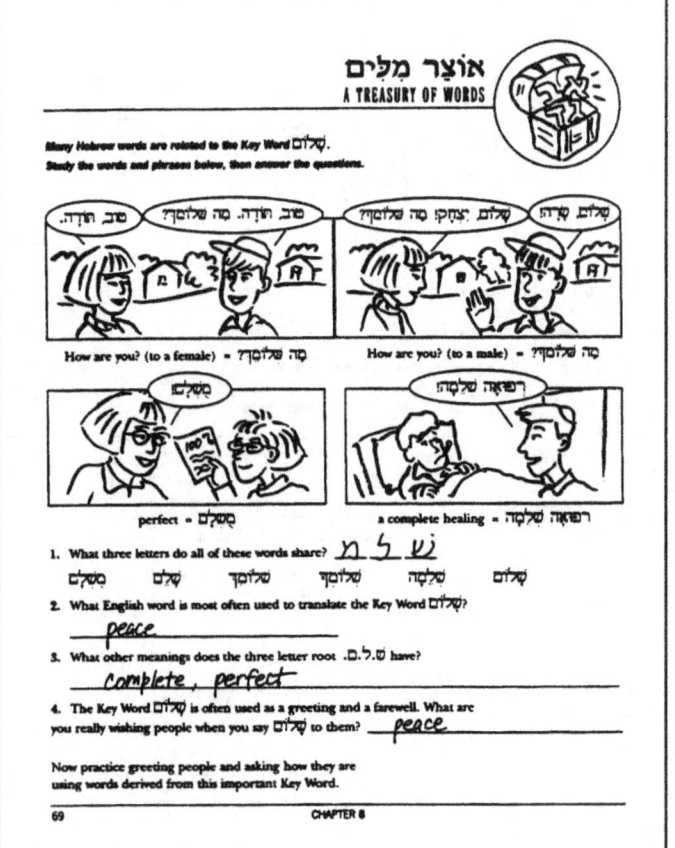

Page 69: Language Enrichment (optional) אוֹצַר מִלִּים

The Key Word שָׁלוֹם may appear to be a simple, straightforward, and easily understood Hebrew term, but such appearances are deceptive. In truth, שָׁלוֹם is one of the richest Jewish value words, and one that is least understood. Most frequently translated as "peace," "hello," or "good-bye," שָׁלוֹם is related to the word שָׁלֵם, meaning "whole" or "complete," as well as to the word מֻשְׁלָם, meaning "perfect." The English word peace is derived from the Latin term Pax, meaning "a treaty to end a war." While a lack of conflict is generic to the Hebrew שָׁלוֹם, Alcalay lists the following additional definitions: quiet, tranquillity, safety, well-being, welfare, contentment, success, and comfort.

Although it is used as both a greeting and a farewell, it does not share a similar derivation to either hello (originally an salutation of good health) or good-bye (a contraction of "God be with ye"). Rather, when used in this manner, שָׁלוֹם is a way of expressing one's hope for another's well-being.

Go over the page with students, then have them complete the page independently. Explain to students that when looking for a three letter root, a letter and its final form are considered to be the same letter, in much the same way that a capital and lower case letter in English are the same letter. Thus, the ם or the מ is the third letter in the root שׁ.ל.מ. This page should be completed by all students, as it deals with the Key Word. For students completing the Language Enrichment component, the word מַה שְׁלוֹמְךָ? is reviewed, and רְפוּאָה שְׁלֵמָה and מַה שְׁלוֹמֵךְ? are new vocabulary, but מֻשְׁלָם will not reappear in the Workbook and is only given to illustrate the meaning of the three letter root שׁ.ל.מ.

Page 70: Language Enrichment (optional)

Introduce orally the new vocabulary (which was first presented on the previous page in the Workbook). Play a game with the greetings. The teacher begins by saying שָׁלוֹם to one student and asking the student either, "מַה שְׁלוֹמְךָ?" or "מַה שְׁלוֹמֵךְ?" The student answers and then repeats the process with another student, until each member of the class has had a turn. This can easily be done as a way of adding Hebrew content to the mundane task of taking attendance.

Read the entire page aloud with students. This is good Hebrew reading practice, and will also make the activity less overwhelming. Have students fill in the answers independently after you have gone over the page.

Page 71: Language Enrichment (optional)
אוֹצָר מִלִּים

Introduce the new pronouns orally. Use an activity similar to that in the Workbook. Give your students new identities. Print their new names in Hebrew on index cards which you tape or pin onto them. The new names can be historical personages, Jewish or secular, or characters from modern culture. Start by making statements about groups of students using the new pronouns. Then ask questions that require other students to use the pronouns in their answers. For more advanced groups, you can make this a guessing game, during which you describe a group of students and ask, "מִי הֵם?" or have the students describe themselves and have others guess, "אַתֶּם ____".

Explain that mixed gender groups use the masculine form of the pronouns, and that only all female groups use the feminine forms.

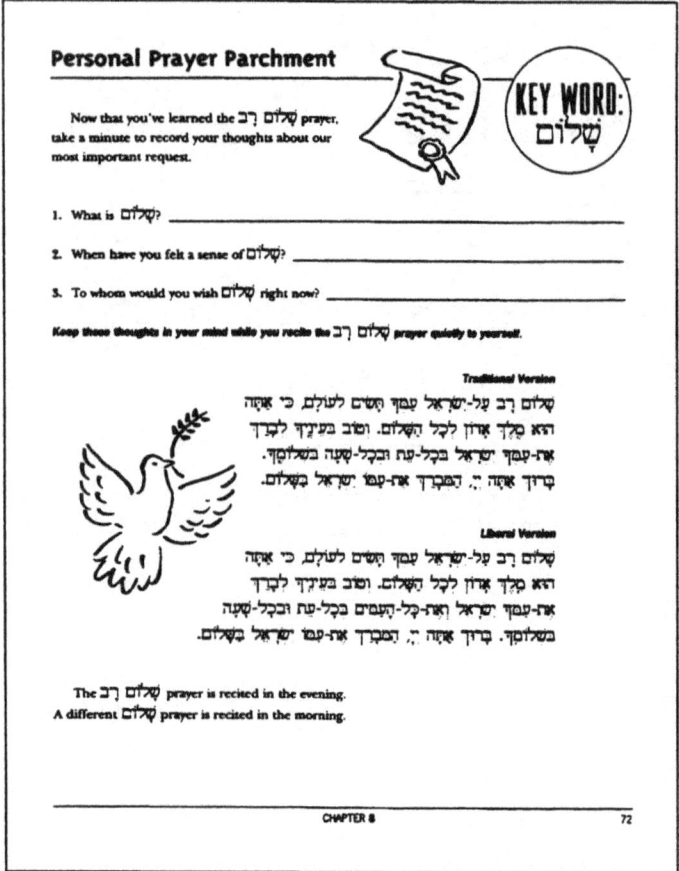

Page 72: Personal Prayer Parchment
Play the game *Broken Squares*. This is one of many games used to build group cooperation skills. Squares of oak tag are cut into eight to ten varied geometric shapes which, when placed together properly, recreate the square. The class is divided into groups of four or five players. One complete set of puzzle pieces is needed per group. Each student is given one piece of the puzzle, one is placed in the center as a foundation, and the remaining pieces are placed in a pile. The goal is for the group to complete its square as quickly as possible (in complete silence). A ten second stoppage of play is instituted any time a member of the team speaks. In turn, each student must try to place his or her piece in its correct place within the puzzle. During a turn, a player may swap a piece for one in the pile of extras. They may not ask one another for a piece, but one student may silently offer to exchange a piece with the player whose turn it is. Play continues for five minutes, or until one team completes its puzzle.

Broken Squares is an excellent metaphor to

employ with the שָׁלוֹם רָב prayer. Because the word שָׁלוֹם denotes not only "peace," but a sense of harmony, wholeness, and completion, the broken pieces represent our world, and the completed square symbolizes that state of perfection we know as שָׁלוֹם. Only through genuine cooperation between people and nations will we be able to achieve this ideal. Discuss these ideas with the students. Ask them how difficult it was to work together, and what strategies they were able to develop during the course of the game. Then recite or chant the שָׁלוֹם רָב prayer together.

Background Information

While the text of שָׁלוֹם רָב is fairly uniform across denominational lines, it is a feature only of the Ashkenazic rite, and is unknown in Sephardic traditions. In Sephardic rite, שָׁלוֹם שִׂים is recited at the end of every עֲמִידָה, while among Ashkenazic Jews, שִׂים שָׁלוֹם is recited only during Shacharit and Musaf services, as well as Minchah on fast days. During the High Holy Days, a short passage asking that we be inscribed in the Book of life, blessing, and peace is inserted just before the concluding benediction, and in Ashkenazic communities, the phrasing of the blessing is changed from הַמְבָרֵךְ אֶת-עַמּוֹ יִשְׂרָאֵל בַּשָּׁלוֹם to עוֹשֵׂה הַשָּׁלוֹם. Sephardim do not change the blessing formula, but recite הַמְבָרֵךְ אֶת-עַמּוֹ יִשְׂרָאֵל בַּשָּׁלוֹם year-round.

Chapter 9 שִׂים שָׁלוֹם

Core Concept: May God Bless You and Keep You.

Key Word: blessing בְּרָכָה

Review Vocabulary Words (optional):

head	רֹאשׁ	big (masc. sing.)	גָּדוֹל
arm, hand	יָד	big (fem. sing.)	גְּדוֹלָה
arms, hands	יָדַיִם	eat (masc. sing.)	אוֹכֵל
tongue (language)	לָשׁוֹן	go, walk (masc. sing.)	הוֹלֵךְ
three	שָׁלוֹשׁ	write (sing.)	כּוֹתֵב / כּוֹתֶבֶת
eight	שְׁמוֹנֶה	study (fem. sing.)	לוֹמֶדֶת
lunch	אֲרוּחַת צָהֳרַיִם	pray (sing.)	מִתְפַּלֵּל / מִתְפַּלֶּלֶת
I have	יֵשׁ לִי	want (sing.)	רוֹצֶה / רוֹצָה
dog	כֶּלֶב	hear (fem. sing.)	שׁוֹמַעַת

New Vocabulary Words (optional):

face	פָּנִים	nose	אַף
mouth	פֶּה	heart	לֵב
eye	עַיִן	leg, foot	רֶגֶל
eyes	עֵינַיִם	legs, feet	רַגְלַיִם
ear	אֹזֶן	I don't have	אֵין לִי
ears	אָזְנַיִם		

New Language Elements (optional):

Use of the infinitive verb form with the verb רוֹצֶה and רוֹצָה.
Construct form (*S'michut*) with plural nouns:

הַפָּנִים + שֶׁלְּךָ = פָּנֶיךָ , הָעֵינַיִם + שֶׁלְּךָ = עֵינֶיךָ

Page 73: May God Bless You and Keep You

This page provides independent reading practice using the prayer text, as well as work with three letter roots. Remind students that a letter and its final form are considered to be the same letter. Tell them also that a letter with or without a dagesh are the same letter (in this case the B and b). After students have completed the page, read over their answers with the whole class, as this provides an additional way to drill the prayer.

The Key Word presented in this chapter, בְּרָכָה, is basic to any understanding of Jewish worship. Often called "the building block of Jewish prayer," the בְּרָכוֹת are so central to Jewish life that a traditional Jew attempts to recite 100 of them each day, in accordance with Rabbi Meir's statement (*Menachot* 43b). בְּרָכוֹת serve several purposes. First, each בְּרָכָה is a reminder that God is the source of all the pleasures of this world. Our Rabbis taught: "It is forbidden for one to enjoy anything of this world without saying a בְּרָכָה, and one who enjoys anything of this world without a benediction commits a sacrilege." (*Berachot* 35a) בְּרָכוֹת are essentially a way of expressing our thanks for God's abundant gifts. Second, blessings act as a focal point. It is difficult to take life for granted if one must be aware of what sights, sounds, smells, or actions require saying a בְּרָכָה. Through the recitation of blessings, we become more sensitive to the beauty and wonder of the world in which we live.

At the same time, the בְּרָכוֹת make a theological statement about God as the Creator and Ruler of the universe, and about our relationship as God's partners in creation. As we thank God for the gifts of this world, we must also acknowledge our responsibility for taking care of them. Finally, reciting a בְּרָכָה infuses even the most ordinary act with a sense of holiness. בְּרָכוֹת deepen our awareness of God's beneficence, while at the same time they transform everyday experience into a great religious adventure in which we, as God's partners, change the ordinary world into the realm of the Divine.

According to the Talmud (*Berachot* 33a), the בְּרָכוֹת were introduced by the Men of the Great

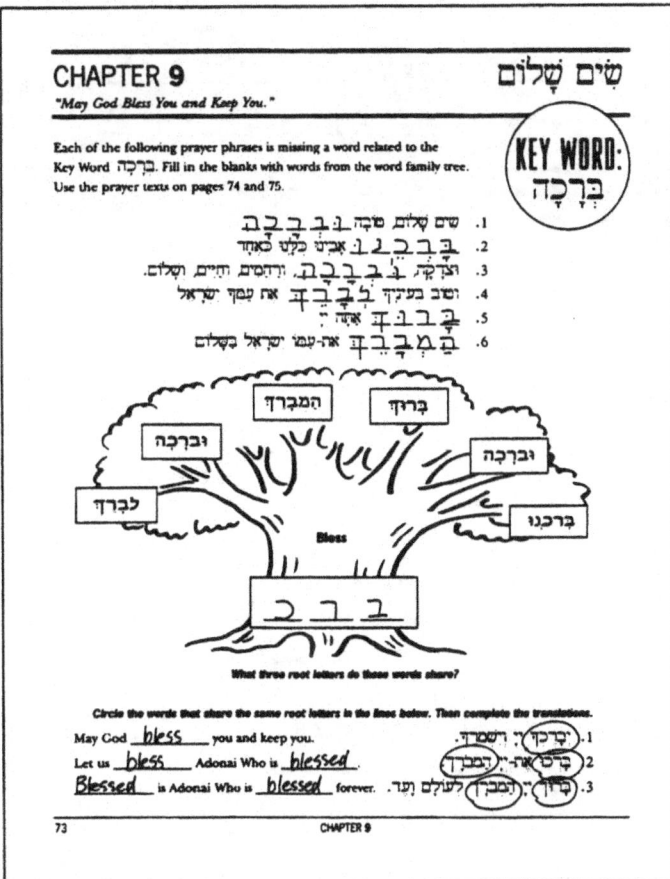

Assembly. Tradition teaches that this Assembly, or Sanhedrin, was established by Ezra, and that among its original 120 members were many prophets. While the Sanhedrin did not "write" the בְּרָכוֹת we use today, they did set the basic structure of synagogue worship and instituted the recitation of בְּרָכוֹת in a fixed form for various occasions. The final form of the בְּרָכוֹת was firmly established by the Talmud. The Key Word activity on page 73 allows students to explore several common forms of the root .בּ.ר.ךְ, and connects it directly to the prayer text.

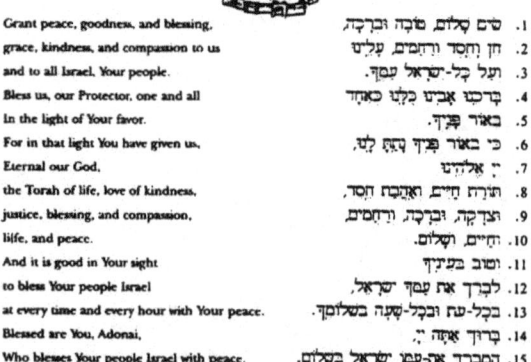

Pages 74-75: The Twelve Gates

Three different versions of the prayer are presented in this chapter. The first is the Ashkenazic Orthodox version, which serves as a basis for comparison. The Conservative and Reform versions of this prayer that are presented here offer a more unambiguously universal outlook, asking God to bless all people with peace. According to the introduction to the 1985 *Siddur Sim Shalom*, Rabbi Jules Harlow explains the origin of the Conservative movement's version of the prayer. Feeling that a more explicit note of universality was needed, the committee adopted the text of שִׂים שָׁלוֹם found in the Siddur of Rabbenu Saadia Gaon (882-942), the first Siddur that included full texts of the prayers.

Similarly, the Liturgy Committee of the Central Conference of American Rabbis, devoted to the development of Reform Siddurim, has created additions that are still more explicitly universal by expanding the phrase,

וְטוֹב בְּעֵינֶיךָ לְבָרֵךְ אֶת עַמְּךָ יִשְׂרָאֵל,

(it is good in Your eyes to bless Your people Israel) to

וְטוֹב בְּעֵינֶיךָ לְבָרֵךְ אֶת עַמְּךָ יִשְׂרָאֵל וְאֶת־כָּל־הָעַמִּים

(it is good in Your eyes to bless Your people Israel and all peoples).

The Orthodox movement felt that the desire for world peace was implicit in the prayer. The task of the Jewish people is to bring שָׁלוֹם, meaning both "peace" and "wholeness, perfection," to the nations of the world as emissaries of monotheism. The necessary prerequisite for this task is that there be שָׁלוֹם, in its full meaning, for the Jewish people.

The Sephardic version of this prayer contains additional minor variations in the text, such as:

שִׂים שָׁלוֹם טוֹבָה וּבְרָכָה חַיִּים חֵן וָחֶסֶד צְדָקָה וְרַחֲמִים

(Grant peace, goodness, and blessing, life, favor, and kindness, justice, and compassion).

Teach students the version of the prayer your congregation uses.

Page 76: Yidbit and Text Exploration

Read through the Yidbit with the class. Since many students will be unfamiliar with the custom of parents blessing children on Friday nights, the Workbook states that "some" parents do this. Your students' families may be interested in learning about and incorporating this ritual, particularly if you emphasize to non-Hebrew reading parents that any words of care and affection are appropriate.

The Text Exploration activity introduces the plural construct form (*S'michut*). The use of the construct form with singular nouns was introduced in Chapter 8 of Book 2 and should be reviewed before introducing the plural form. This can easily be incorporated into a review of the וְאָהַבְתָּ, an important prayer to review.

Read the opening sentence, and ask students to focus on the words: נַפְשְׁךָ, and מְאֹדֶךָ, לְבָבְךָ. Write the base words, לֵב (heart), נֶפֶשׁ (soul), and מְאֹד (very much; in ancient times, wealth) on the board. Elicit their meanings from the students, and ask what has been added to these terms in the prayer text, and what that particle means. Then introduce the plural form using the two examples from the שִׂים שָׁלוֹם prayer text. Explain the new concept, that the letter י is an indication of the plural. Then write the words שְׁעָרִים (gates) and בָּנִים (children, sons) on the board. Again, elicit their meanings from the students, then ask them to return to the text of the וְאָהַבְתָּ, and to locate the examples of the new form of these words that are found in the text: וּבִשְׁעָרֶיךָ (and on your gates), and לְבָנֶיךָ (to your children). Finally, read through the entire וְאָהַבְתָּ.

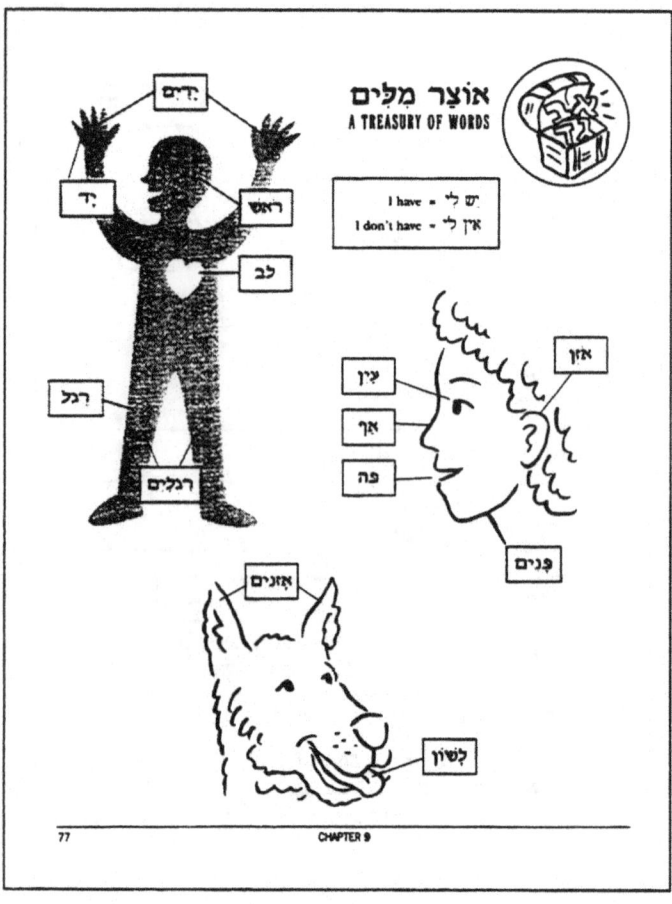

Pages 77-78: Language Enrichment (optional)
אוֹצַר מִלִים

Introduce the new vocabulary orally. Although it appears to be a large number of new words to introduce at the same time, some of the words on the page are review, and others are simply plural forms. The vocabulary is tied to the prayer text because the Hebrew words for face and eyes occur in the prayer text. Introduce the words by playing a game similar to *Simon Says*. Standing in front of the class, touch or move a body part as you say what you're doing, and have students repeat both your words and motions. Then give oral instructions without using the hand movements, and have students continue to repeat your words, and independently perform the body motion. After they become more proficient, play the Hebrew version of *Simon Says*, שִׁמְעוֹן אוֹמֵר. Since you do not want students who are "out" to sit passively, let those students who wish to do so give the instructions, rather than the winner of the game. Alternately, you can continue giving instructions without eliminating anyone. In this case, either note who has gotten confused, or ignore the whole issue of winning altogether.

Go over the sentences on page 78 after you have introduced the vocabulary. Then students can complete the pages independently in class or for homework.

Pages 79-80: Language Enrichment (optional)

Students will probably not have difficulty with the new language concept of infinitives, since they are formed in Hebrew similarly to how they are formed in English, by adding the prefix meaning "to" in front of the verb. In Hebrew the verb itself also changes, but in the examples chosen here, the verb is still recognizable. Students were introduced to the verb רוֹצֶה / רוֹצָה in Chapter 7. Now, it is used together with the infinitive verb. Again, this is similar to English (unlike the word "can" which is used with an infinitive only in Hebrew, leading to many errors for beginning language learners).

Teach the new concept with a demonstration. Choose students (both boys and girls) to act out the verbs that appear on page 79 of the Workbook. As each student silently performs, state the action that he or she is doing, or call on students to describe the action, for example, "שָׂרָה כּוֹתֶבֶת." Then, ask for volunteers who also want to act out the verbs, by using the new form, for example, "מִי רוֹצֶה לִכְתֹּב?" Note that the correct way of asking this type of question will always use the masculine form (unless there are only girls present) since the assumption is that either a male or female might respond. If you want to drill the female form, רוֹצָה, then be sure to acknowledge girls that volunteer by answering their requests with questions such as, "אַתְּ רוֹצָה לִכְתֹּב?"

Go over all the sentences on page 80 before having students complete the page independently. This provides an extra opportunity for reading practice, and helps students who are overwhelmed by the amount of Hebrew vocabulary and reading.

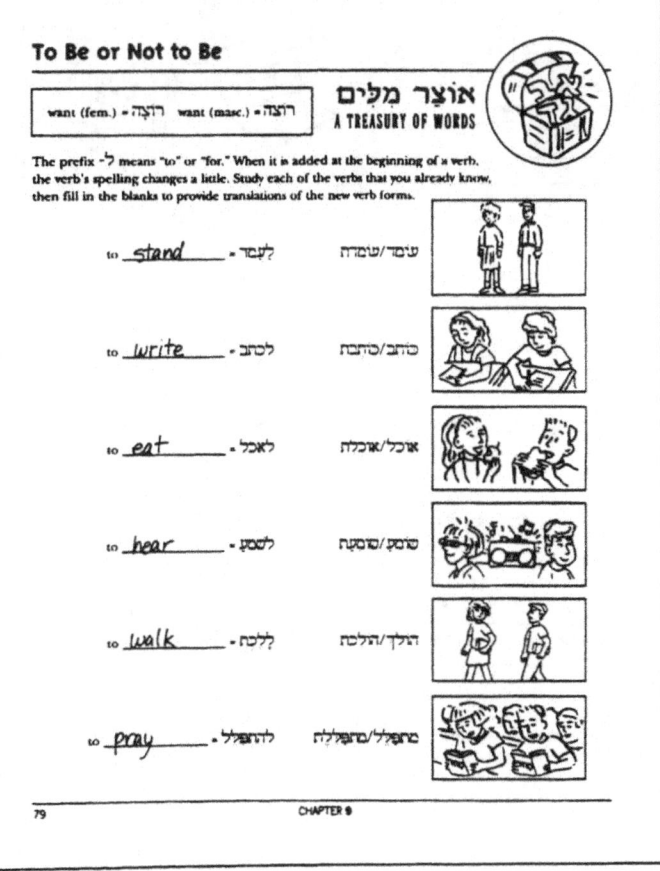

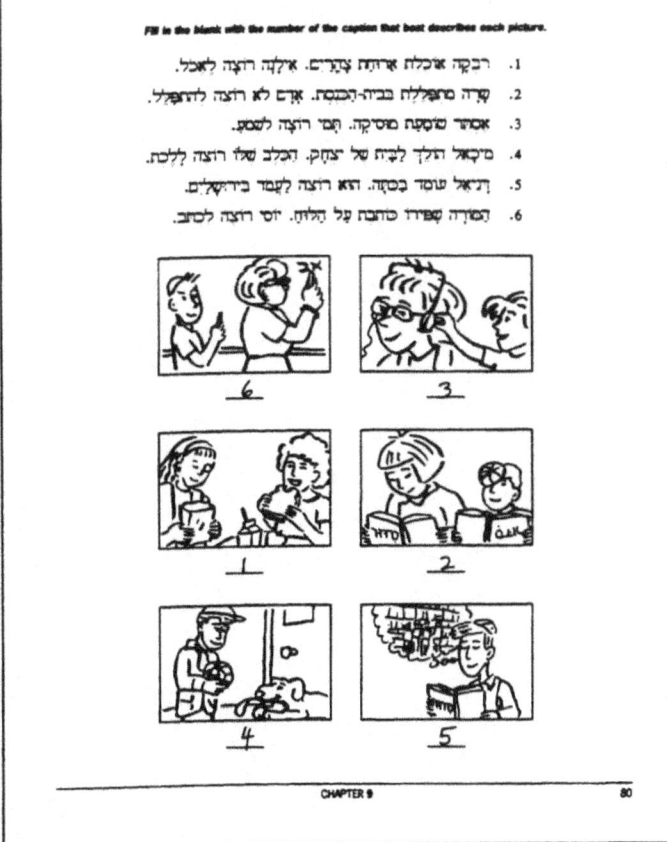

Page 81: Personal Prayer Parchment

As a variation to the game *Broken Squares*, create a jigsaw puzzle using the pre-cut blank puzzles that are commercially available from educational supply companies. On each piece, write one of the words that appears in the שִׂים שָׁלוֹם text, (i.e., צְדָקָה, חֵן, חֶסֶד, שָׁלוֹם, בְּרָכָה, רַחֲמִים, etc.). After students complete the puzzles, discuss why each element is necessary to creating true שָׁלוֹם. You can explain in English the concepts that are unfamiliar to students. Then recite or chant the prayer as a class.

Background Information

Like the עֲבוֹדָה and the הוֹדָאָה, the שִׂים שָׁלוֹם is derived from the ancient Temple service. When the sacrifices had been offered, and the prayer of thanksgiving recited, the *Kohanim* would bless the people by uttering the "three-fold," or priestly blessing. Traditional congregations incorporate this blessing during the repetition of the עֲמִידָה, as an introduction to שִׂים שָׁלוֹם. In some communities, the *Kohanim*, modern descendants of the ancient priests, continue to come forward to bless the congregation during Festival services in a ritual known as *Dukhan*. The inclusion of the priestly blessing is discussed in the Yidbit on page 76.

Chapter 10 אֱלֹהַי נְצוֹר

Core Concept: May God Guard My Tongue from Evil.

Key Word: tongue לָשׁוֹן

Review Vocabulary Words (optional):

letter	מִכְתָּב	with	עִם
head	רֹאשׁ	on	עַל
brother	אָח	stand (masc. sing.)	עוֹמֵד
dinner	אֲרוּחַת עֶרֶב	give (fem. sing.)	נוֹתֶנֶת
my	שֶׁלִּי		

New Vocabulary Words (optional):

do, make (masc. sing.)	עוֹשֶׂה	do, make (fem. sing.)	עוֹשָׂה

Review Language Elements (optional):
Singular present tense verbs

Page 82: May God Guard My Tongue from Evil

Teach students to read the prayer accurately, but if students will not be expected to recite it aloud, it is not necessary to teach for fluency. However, lines 19-22 should be mastered by all students, as the verse עֹשֶׂה שָׁלוֹם is such an important one in Jewish liturgy.

Pages 83-84: Like Feathers in the Wind

Read the story together with the class. After Ilana, Michael, and Rebecca give their opinions on Yossi's predicament (and before Mrs. Shapiro calls them to task), ask your students to give their opinions on what has happened to Yossi. Chances are that your students will agree with Mrs. Shapiro's students, accusing Yossi of all sorts of wrongdoing. Then finish reading the story. Talk to your students about how easy it is to fall into the trap of gossiping about people or judging someone unfavorably. Even though the Yossi that they "gossiped" about is a fictional character, how different is the way they talked about him from the way they talk about each other? Come up with a class plan to work on the לָשׁוֹן הָרָע issue. One often used technique is to have everyone (including the teacher!) choose an hour a day when they will make a special effort not to speak about others. Those who want a challenge should pick a time when they know they have a tendency to gossip, perhaps an evening hour when they usually chat on the phone. (No one is allowed to choose an hour when they're asleep!) After a week, have everyone report back about their efforts. Even acknowledging that they failed to control their speech is an extremely valuable learning experience, as students will have increased their awareness of the issue. Incidentally, לְשׁוֹן הָרַע is a major cause of social friction among preteens, so this is an excellent issue to tackle, not only because of its Jewish significance. Students this age are constantly embroiled in "He told me that you said to his friend that she . . . " type of arguments.

The Key Word לָשׁוֹן is another excellent example of how figurative use can extend the meanings of words for physical items. Just as the English word "tongue" has come to represent language in general, the Hebrew word לָשׁוֹן (tongue) has developed the same figurative use. The similarity between the two, however, ends there, as the Hebrew term לָשׁוֹן has also come to stand for the ethical uses of speech as well. In Jewish thought, language is far more than just talking. It holds the power to create worlds. The Torah teaches that God created the world through ten utterances. By simply saying, "Let there be . . . ," God brought the entire universe into being. Hebrew, traditionally held as the language of creation as well as Jewish worship and scholarship, is thus known as לְשׁוֹן הַקֹּדֶשׁ. In the Jerusalem Talmud, Rabbi Meir teaches that speaking the לְשׁוֹן הַקֹּדֶשׁ in conjunction with living in the Land of Israel, and reciting the שְׁמַע evening and morning, assures one a place in the world to come. While the sages always viewed Hebrew as a form of protection against assimilation, linguists in our own day have noted the power of language to inform our perceptions, views, and experiences, and to bind us to our culture.

While language can have the power to do great good, it can also be used for extremely destructive purposes. In Hebrew, the term לְשׁוֹן הָרַע is used to describe evil uses of speech, especially slander. The Rabbis considered לְשׁוֹן הָרַע to be a heinous crime, on a moral par with murder and idolatry. The paragraph that ends the עֲמִידָה (אֱלֹהַי נְצוֹר) discusses both

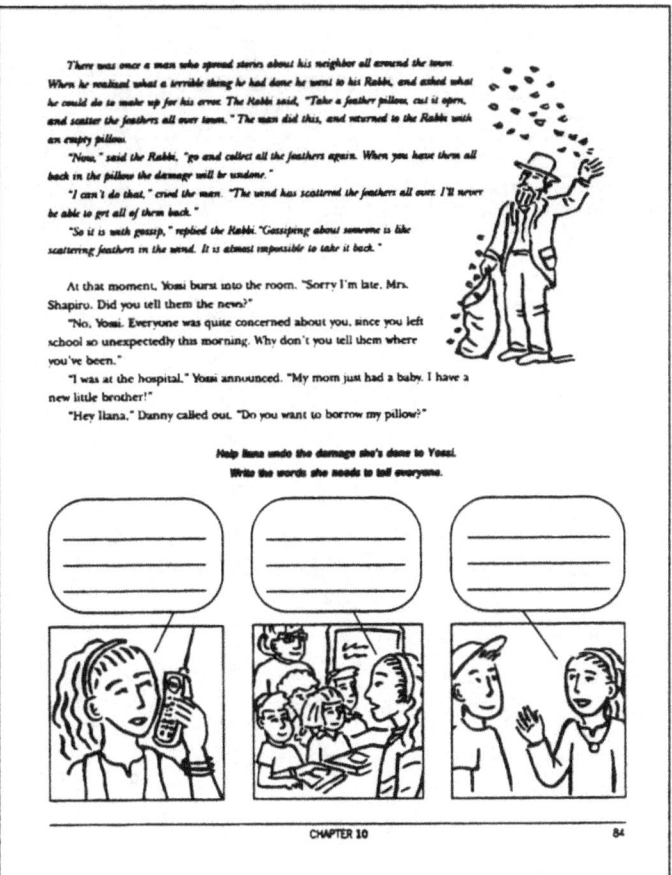

aspects of the power of language. First, it asks God to help us use our speech for good rather than evil purposes. Then it asks God to annul the plans and decrees of those who think, and therefore might speak, ill of us.

Page 85: Language Enrichment (optional)
אוֹצַר מִלִים

The new verb עוֹשֶׂה appears in the prayer text. You will probably need to translate the verb, but then present it orally before doing the Workbook page. Use pictures of people engaged in a variety of activities, or have students act out various activities. Ask questions such as, "מַה הִיא עוֹשָׂה?" or "מַה אַתָּה עוֹשֶׂה?". Using nine pictures, play a tick-tack-toe game. Tape or stick the pictures on the blackboard in three rows of three each. Divide the class into two teams. In order to mark a square as X or O, two members of a team must correctly ask and answer a question about what the person in the picture is doing. For example, two teammates choose a picture of a boy listening to music. One asks the question, "מַה הוּא עוֹשֶׂה?" The other answers, "הוּא שׁוֹמֵעַ מוּסִיקָה." If either the question or answer is incorrect, the team does not get that square, and the other team has its turn. Having two students asking and answering is more realistic linguistically (after all, we usually have other people answer our questions), and it also provides a way of using the new verb and involving more students actively in the game.

Page 86: Yidbit

The name verses for students are found in Appendix 1 on page 90 of this Teacher Guide. In addition, students can use any verse that contains their entire name.

You can photocopy the blank emblem on colored paper and have students design emblems for a class bulletin board.

Page 87: Prayerobics

Teach the steps to the conclusion of the prayer if they are used by your congregation. If not, have students try to use the steps in a class worship service. These movements are a little more complicated; students may need to practice them several times in order to feel comfortable.

Page 88: Personal Prayer Parchment

Tell the class the following story about Shmuel HaNaggid. Not only one of the leading Rabbis and poets of the Golden Age of Spain, he eventually rose to become the Vizier (second in command) to the Caliph in Granada. This story was included in a letter of condolence that Shmuel HaNaggid sent to Rabbaynu Chananel on the death of his father.

I was riding with Caliph Habbas at the head of a procession, with his sons and the nobility following behind. Barriers had been set up along the road to protect the royal procession. Suddenly, a well-known merchant came through the barrier, jumped over the ropes, and began to curse me. The Caliph was furious. He said, "That man has no call to use his tongue for such evil purposes! He cannot insult my minister without paying for his actions," and he ordered me to have the merchant's tongue cut out.

When we returned to the palace, I ordered the merchant to appear before me. He arrived, fearful, anxious, and expecting the worst. I told him that I would not harm him physically so long as he regretted his action and promised never to curse anyone ever again.

The following year, the Caliph and I again led the procession of his court. The merchant again came forward as the Caliph's coach approached. But this time he bowed deeply and called out, "Allah be praised! May the God of Vizier Shmuel be blessed!" Then he jumped behind the barrier.

The Caliph turned to me and said, "Did I not order you to cut out that man's tongue?"

"Your majesty," I answered. "I surely did obey your order! I cut out that man's evil tongue and replaced it with a good one!"

After telling the story, ask the students to close their eyes, and think about a similar experience they might have had. Direct them to think about how they could follow Shmuel HaNaggid's example to turn a potential enemy into a friend. After a couple of minutes, ask the students to open their eyes, and recite the prayer together.

As an alternative, divide the class into teams, and hold a "שָׁלוֹם Song Sing-Down." In this activity, each team in turn is asked to sing a melody for each of the following prayers: שָׁלוֹם רָב, שִׂים שָׁלוֹם, and עֹשֶׂה שָׁלוֹם. A point is awarded for each new melody. Additional points can be awarded for creative melodies or those that are less common. The teams take turns until none of them can come up with an additional melody during its turn. The team that has the greatest number of points wins the game.

Background Information

Since Talmudic times, it has been customary to add a personal meditation at the end of the עֲמִידָה in order to add an element of spontaneity to the fixed prayer composed by the Sages of the Great Assembly. The Talmud cites 11 sages and provides the texts of their personal meditations for the end of the עֲמִידָה, (see *Berachot* 16b-17a). Of these, the אֱלֹהַי נְצוֹר has been selected to end the עֲמִידָה in most prayer books.

Written by the fourth century scholar Mar bar Ravina, the text contains a plea that God will help us to make our speech worthy, while also granting protection from those who would speak ill of us. The text presented in the Talmud ends with the passage:

וְכֹל הַחוֹשְׁבִים עָלַי רָעָה מְהֵרָה
הָפֵר עֲצָתָם וְקַלְקֵל מַחְשַׁבְתָּם.

(And those who think evil about me, speedily annul their plots and spoil their plans.) The next four phrases were added later to ensure that one's prayers would be answered.

The Talmud (*Berachot* 9b) ordained that the recitation of the עֲמִידָה should be followed immediately with the quotation from Psalm 19:15:

יִהְיוּ לְרָצוֹן אִמְרֵי פִי, וְהֶגְיוֹן לִבִּי לְפָנֶיךָ,
יְיָ צוּרִי וְגוֹאֲלִי.

(May the words of my mouth, and the meditations of my heart be acceptable to You, Adonai, my Rock and my Redeemer.) Prior to this line, it is customary to add one's personal "signature" by reciting the verse from scripture that begins with the first letter and ends with the last letter of one's name.

Following the verse from Psalm 19, the עֲמִידָה concludes with a paraphrasing of Job 25:2:

עֹשֶׂה שָׁלוֹם בִּמְרוֹמָיו, הוּא יַעֲשֶׂה שָׁלוֹם
עָלֵינוּ וְעַל כָּל יִשְׂרָאֵל. וְאִמְרוּ אָמֵן.

(May the One Who makes peace in the heavens, make peace for us and for all Israel. And let us say, Amen.) While reciting this line, it is customary to take one's formal leave from God's royal court by taking three small steps backward, bowing to the left, to the right, and then to the center.

REVIEW PAGES

Page 89: עֲמִידָה Wrap-Up

This type of classification activity involves higher level thinking skills. For some of the prayers, it is quite difficult to determine whether praise, petition, or thanksgiving is the central motif. For example, the עֲבוֹדָה prayer is considered to be a prayer of thanksgiving, as we are thanking God for the opportunity to worship. Do not place too much emphasis on correct answers. Instead, emphasize the process of students coming to their own conclusions.

Page 90: Key Word Word Search

Review the ten Key Words with the class before assigning this page. The answers circled in the puzzle will spell out the Hebrew word תּוֹרָה.

Page 91: Mrs. Shapiro's Bulletin Board

Review all the vocabulary taught in the Workbook. Make sure students have completed the Dictionary on pages 92-95 in the Workbook. Bring in a Poloraid camera and take pictures for a class bulletin board of your students doing a variety of activities. Each student can write a Hebrew caption for their own picture, or for a friend's. Celebrate your completion of the book with a סִיוּם, a traditional celebration honoring the end of a unit of Jewish study.

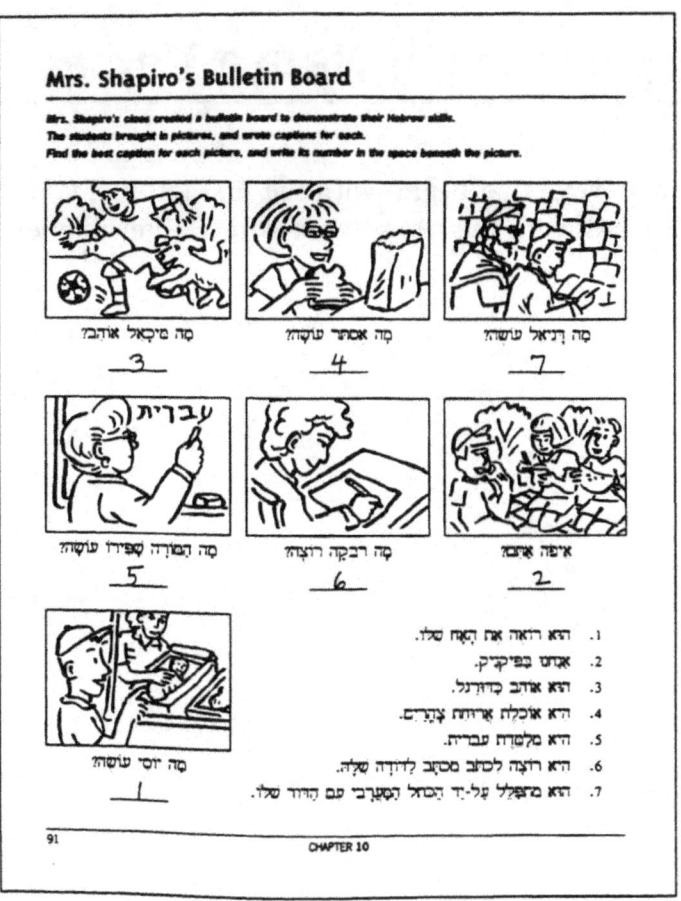

Appendix 1: Name Verses

Find a verse that begins with the first letter of your Hebrew name,
and ends with the last letter of your Hebrew name.

א...א   אָנָּא יהוה הוֹשִׁיעָה נָּא, אָנָּא יהוה הַצְלִיחָה נָּא. (Psalm 118:25)

א...ה   אַשְׁרֵי מַשְׂכִּיל אֶל דָּל, בְּיוֹם רָעָה יְמַלְּטֵהוּ יהוה. (Psalm 41:2)

א...ו   אַשְׁרֵי שֶׁאֵל יַעֲקֹב בְּעֶזְרוֹ, שִׂבְרוֹ עַל יהוה אֱלֹהָיו. (Psalm 146:5)

א...י   אֲמָרַי הַאֲזִינָה יהוה בִּינָה הֲגִיגִי. (Psalm 5:2)

א...ך   אָמַרְתְּ לַיהוה אֲדֹנָי אָתָּה, טוֹבָתִי בַּל עָלֶיךָ. (Psalm 16:2)

א...ל   אֶרֶץ רָעָשָׁה אַף שָׁמַיִם נָטְפוּ מִפְּנֵי אֱלֹהִים זֶה סִינַי, מִפְּנֵי אֱלֹהִים אֱלֹהֵי יִשְׂרָאֵל. (Psalm 68:9)

א...ם   אַתָּה הוּא יהוה הָאֱלֹהִים, אֲשֶׁר בָּחַרְתָּ בְּאַבְרָם, וְהוֹצֵאתוֹ מֵאוּר כַּשְׂדִּים, וְשַׂמְתָּ שְּׁמוֹ אַבְרָהָם. (Nehemiah 9:7)

א...ן   אֵלֶיךָ יהוה אֶקְרָא, וְאֶל אֲדֹנָי אֶתְחַנָּן. (Psalm 30:9)

א...ע   אָמַר בְּלִבּוֹ בַּל אֶמּוֹט, לְדֹר וָדֹר אֲשֶׁר לֹא בְרָע. (Psalm 10:6)

א...ר   אֵלֶּה בָרֶכֶב וְאֵלֶּה בַסּוּסִים, וַאֲנַחְנוּ בְּשֵׁם יהוה אֱלֹהֵינוּ נַזְכִּיר. (Psalm 20:8)

ב...א   בְּרִיתִי הָיְתָה אִתּוֹ הַחַיִּים וְהַשָּׁלוֹם, וָאֶתְּנֵם לוֹ מוֹרָא וַיִּירָאֵנִי, וּמִפְּנֵי שְׁמִי נִחַת הוּא. (Malachi 2:5)

ב...ה   בַּעֲבוּר יִשְׁמְרוּ חֻקָּיו, וְתוֹרֹתָיו יִנְצֹרוּ, הַלְלוּיָהּ. (Psalm 105:45)

ב...ז   בְּיוֹם קָרָאתִי וַתַּעֲנֵנִי, תַּרְהִבֵנִי בְנַפְשִׁי עֹז. (Psalm 138:3)

ב...ך   בָּרוּךְ אַתָּה יהוה, לַמְּדֵנִי חֻקֶּיךָ. (Psalm 119:12)

ב...ל   בְּמַקְהֵלוֹת בָּרְכוּ אֱלֹהִים, אֲדֹנָי מִמְּקוֹר יִשְׂרָאֵל. (Psalm 68:27)

ב...ן   בָּרוּךְ יהוה אֱלֹהֵי יִשְׂרָאֵל מֵהָעוֹלָם וְעַד הָעוֹלָם, אָמֵן וְאָמֵן. (Psalm 41:14)

ב...ע   בְּחֶסֶד וֶאֱמֶת יְכֻפַּר עָוֹן, וּבְיִרְאַת יהוה סוּר מֵרָע. (Proverbs 16:6)

ג...ה   גּוֹל עַל יהוה דַּרְכֶּךָ, וּבְטַח עָלָיו וְהוּא יַעֲשֶׂה. (Psalm 37:5)

ג...ל   גַּם אֲנִי אוֹדְךָ בִכְלִי נֶבֶל, אֲמִתְּךָ אֱלֹהָי, אֲזַמְּרָה לְךָ בְכִנּוֹר, קְדוֹשׁ יִשְׂרָאֵל. (Psalm 71:22)

ג...ן   גַּם בְּנֵי אָדָם גַּם בְּנֵי אִישׁ, יַחַד עָשִׁיר וְאֶבְיוֹן. (Psalm 49:3)

ד...ב   דִּרְשׁוּ יהוה בְּהִמָּצְאוֹ, קְרָאֻהוּ בִּהְיוֹתוֹ קָרוֹב. (Isaiah 55:6)

ד...ד   דִּרְשׁוּ יהוה וְעֻזּוֹ, בַּקְּשׁוּ פָנָיו תָּמִיד. (Psalm 105:4)

ד...ה   דְּאָגָה בְלֶב אִישׁ יַשְׁחֶנָּה, וְדָבָר טוֹב יְשַׂמְּחֶנָּה. (Proverbs 12:25)

ד...ל   דָּן יָדִין עַמּוֹ, כְּאַחַד שִׁבְטֵי יִשְׂרָאֵל. (Genesis 49:16)

ה...א	הַצּוּר תָּמִים פָּעֳלוֹ, כִּי כָל דְּרָכָיו מִשְׁפָּט, אֵל אֱמוּנָה וְאֵין עָוֶל, צַדִּיק וְיָשָׁר הוּא. (Deuteronomy 32:4)
ה...ה	הַסְתֵּר פָּנֶיךָ מֵחֲטָאָי, וְכָל עֲוֺנֹתַי מְחֵה. (Psalm 51:11)
ה...ל	הַקְשִׁיבָה לְקוֹל שַׁוְעִי מַלְכִּי וֵאלֹהָי, כִּי אֵלֶיךָ אֶתְפַּלָּל. (Psalm 5:3)
ז...ב	זֵכֶר צַדִּיק לִבְרָכָה, וְשֵׁם רְשָׁעִים יִרְקָב. (Proverbs 10:7)
ז...ה	זֹאת מְנוּחָתִי עֲדֵי עַד, פֹּה אֵשֵׁב כִּי אִוִּתִיהָ. (Psalm 132:14)
ז...ח	זָכַרְתִּי יָמִים מִקֶּדֶם, הָגִיתִי בְכָל פָּעֳלֶךָ, בְּמַעֲשֵׂה יָדֶיךָ אֲשׂוֹחֵחַ. (Psalm 143:5)
ז...ן	זְבוּלֻן לְחוֹף יַמִּים יִשְׁכֹּן, וְהוּא לְחוֹף אֳנִיּוֹת וְיַרְכָתוֹ עַל צִידֹן. (Genesis 49:13)
ח...ה	חָגְרָה בְעוֹז מָתְנֶיהָ, וַתְּאַמֵּץ זְרוֹעֹתֶיהָ. (Proverbs 31:17)
ח...ך	חֲצוֹת לַיְלָה אָקוּם לְהוֹדוֹת לָךְ, עַל מִשְׁפְּטֵי צִדְקֶךָ. (Psalm 119:62)
ח...ם	חֹנֶה מַלְאַךְ יְהוָה סָבִיב לִירֵאָיו, וַיְחַלְּצֵם. (Psalm 34:8)
ט...א	טוֹב יַנְחִיל בְּנֵי בָנִים, וְצָפוּן לַצַּדִּיק חֵיל חוֹטֵא. (Proverbs 13:22)
ט...ה	טָמְנוּ גֵאִים פַּח לִי, וַחֲבָלִים פָּרְשׂוּ רֶשֶׁת לְיַד מַעְגָּל, מֹקְשִׁים שָׁתוּ לִי סֶלָה. (Psalm 140:6)
י...א	יִשְׂרָאֵל בְּטַח בַּיהוָה עֶזְרָם וּמָגִנָּם הוּא. (Psalm 115:9)
י...ב	יַעַנְךָ יְהוָה בְּיוֹם צָרָה, יְשַׂגֶּבְךָ שֵׁם אֱלֹהֵי יַעֲקֹב. (Psalm 20:2)
י...ד	יָסַד אֶרֶץ עַל מְכוֹנֶיהָ, בַּל תִּמּוֹט עוֹלָם וָעֶד. (Psalm 104:5)
י...ה	יְהוָה הַצִּילָה נַפְשִׁי מִשְּׂפַת שֶׁקֶר, מִלָּשׁוֹן רְמִיָּה. (Psalm 120:2)
י...י	יְהוָה לִי בְּעֹזְרָי, וַאֲנִי אֶרְאֶה בְשֹׂנְאָי. (Psalm 118:7)
י...ל	יְמִין יְהוָה רוֹמֵמָה, יְמִין יְהוָה עֹשָׂה חָיִל. (Psalm 118:16)
י...ם	יַעְלְזוּ חֲסִידִים בְּכָבוֹד, יְרַנְּנוּ עַל מִשְׁכְּבוֹתָם. (Psalm 149:5)
י...ן	יָשֵׂם נְהָרוֹת לְמִדְבָּר, וּמֹצָאֵי מַיִם לְצִמָּאוֹן. (Psalm 107:33)
י...ע	יָחֹס עַל דַּל וְאֶבְיוֹן, וְנַפְשׁוֹת אֶבְיוֹנִים יוֹשִׁיעַ. (Psalm 72:13)
י...ף	יְהוָה יִגְמֹר בַּעֲדִי, יְהוָה חַסְדְּךָ לְעוֹלָם, מַעֲשֵׂי יָדֶיךָ אַל תֶּרֶף. (Psalm 138:8)
י...ץ	יְבָרְכֵנוּ אֱלֹהִים וְיִירְאוּ אוֹתוֹ כָּל אַפְסֵי אָרֶץ. (Psalm 67:8)
י...ק	יוֹצִיאֵם מֵחֹשֶׁךְ וְצַלְמָוֶת, וּמוֹסְרוֹתֵיהֶם יְנַתֵּק. (Psalm 107:14)
י...ר	יְהוָה שִׁמְךָ לְעוֹלָם, יְהוָה זִכְרְךָ לְדֹר וָדֹר. (Psalm 135:13)
י...ת	יְהוָה שֹׁמֵר אֶת גֵּרִים, יָתוֹם וְאַלְמָנָה יְעוֹדֵד, וְדֶרֶךְ רְשָׁעִים יְעַוֵּת. (Psalm 146:9)
כ...ב	כִּי לֹא יִטֹּשׁ יְהוָה עַמּוֹ, וְנַחֲלָתוֹ לֹא יַעֲזֹב. (Psalm 94:14)
כ...ל	כִּי מֶלֶךְ כָּל הָאָרֶץ אֱלֹהִים, זַמְּרוּ מַשְׂכִּיל. (Psalm 47:8)
ל...א	לֹא תִהְיֶה מְשַׁכֵּלָה וַעֲקָרָה בְּאַרְצֶךָ, אֶת מִסְפַּר יָמֶיךָ אֲמַלֵּא. (Exodus 23:26)
ל...ה	לְדָוִד בָּרוּךְ יְהוָה צוּרִי הַמְלַמֵּד יָדַי לַקְרָב, אֶצְבְּעוֹתַי לַמִּלְחָמָה. (Psalm 144:1)
ל...י	לוּלֵי תוֹרָתְךָ שַׁעֲשֻׁעָי, אָז אָבַדְתִּי בְעָנְיִי. (Psalm 119:92)

ל	לַמְנַצֵּחַ עַל שֹׁשַׁנִּים לִבְנֵי קֹרַח, מַשְׂכִּיל שִׁיר יְדִידֹת. (Psalm 45:1)	ת...
מ	מִי כָמֹכָה בָּאֵלִם יהוה מִי כָּמֹכָה נֶאְדָּר בַּקֹּדֶשׁ, נוֹרָא תְהִלֹּת עֹשֵׂה פֶלֶא. (Exodus 15:11)	א...
מ	מַחֲשָׁבוֹת בְּעֵצָה תִכּוֹן, וּבְתַחְבֻּלוֹת עֲשֵׂה מִלְחָמָה. (Proverbs 20:18)	ה...
מ	מַה דּוֹדֵךְ מִדּוֹד הַיָּפָה בַּנָּשִׁים, מַה דּוֹדֵךְ מִדּוֹד שֶׁכָּכָה הִשְׁבַּעְתָּנוּ. (Song of Songs 5:9)	ו...
מ	מָה אָהַבְתִּי תוֹרָתֶךָ, כָּל הַיּוֹם הִיא שִׂיחָתִי. (Psalm 119:97)	י...
מ	מַה טֹּבוּ אֹהָלֶיךָ יַעֲקֹב, מִשְׁכְּנֹתֶיךָ יִשְׂרָאֵל. (Numbers 24:5)	ל...
מ	מְאוֹר עֵינַיִם יְשַׂמַּח לֵב, שְׁמוּעָה טוֹבָה תְּדַשֶּׁן עָצֶם. (Proverbs 15:30)	ם...
מ	מִי זֶה הָאִישׁ יְרֵא יהוה, יוֹרֶנּוּ בְּדֶרֶךְ יִבְחָר. (Psalm 25:12)	ר...
נ	נַפְשֵׁנוּ חִכְּתָה לַיהוה, עֶזְרֵנוּ וּמָגִנֵּנוּ הוּא. (Psalm 33:20)	א...
נ	נָחַלְתִּי עֵדְוֹתֶיךָ לְעוֹלָם, כִּי שְׂשׂוֹן לִבִּי הֵמָּה. (Psalm 119:111)	ה...
נ	נִדְבוֹת פִּי רְצֵה נָא יהוה, וּמִשְׁפָּטֶיךָ לַמְּדֵנִי. (Psalm 119:108)	י...
נ	נֶחְשַׁבְתִּי עִם יוֹרְדֵי בוֹר, הָיִיתִי כְּגֶבֶר אֵין אֱיָל. (Psalm 88:5)	ל...
נ	נַחֲמוּ נַחֲמוּ עַמִּי, יֹאמַר אֱלֹהֵיכֶם. (Isaiah 40:1)	ם...
נ	נֵר יהוה נִשְׁמַת אָדָם, חֹפֵשׂ כָּל חַדְרֵי בָטֶן. (Proverbs 20:27)	ן...
ס	סֹבּוּ צִיּוֹן וְהַקִּיפוּהָ סִפְרוּ מִגְדָּלֶיהָ. (Psalm 48:13)	ה...
ס	סֵעֲפִים שָׂנֵאתִי, וְתוֹרָתְךָ אָהָבְתִּי. (Psalm 119:113)	י...
ע	עַתָּה אָקוּם, יֹאמַר יהוה, עַתָּה אֵרוֹמָם, עַתָּה אֶנָּשֵׂא. (Isaiah 33:10)	א...
ע	עַד אֶמְצָא מָקוֹם לַיהוה, מִשְׁכָּנוֹת לַאֲבִיר יַעֲקֹב. (Psalm 132:5)	ב...
ע	עָזִּי וְזִמְרָת יָהּ, וַיְהִי לִי לִישׁוּעָה. (Psalm 118:14)	ה...
ע	עַל דַּעְתְּךָ כִּי לֹא אֶרְשָׁע, וְאֵין מִיָּדְךָ מַצִּיל. (Job 10:7)	ל...
ע	עֲרֹב עַבְדְּךָ לְטוֹב, אַל יַעַשְׁקֻנִי זֵדִים. (Psalm 119:122)	ם...
ע	עֹשֶׂה גְדֹלוֹת וְאֵין חֵקֶר, נִפְלָאוֹת עַד אֵין מִסְפָּר. (Job 5:9)	ר...
פ	פִּתְחוּ לִי שַׁעֲרֵי צֶדֶק, אָבֹא בָם אוֹדֶה יָהּ. (Psalm 118:19)	ה...
פ	פֶּן יִטְרֹף כְּאַרְיֵה נַפְשִׁי, פֹּרֵק וְאֵין מַצִּיל. (Psalm 7:3)	ל...
פ	פֶּלֶס וּמֹאזְנֵי מִשְׁפָּט לַיהוה, מַעֲשֵׂהוּ כָּל אַבְנֵי כִיס. (Proverbs 16:11)	ס...
פ	פִּנִּיתָ לְפָנֶיהָ וַתַּשְׁרֵשׁ שָׁרָשֶׁיהָ וַתְּמַלֵּא אָרֶץ. (Psalm 80:10)	ץ...
צ	צִיּוֹן בְּמִשְׁפָּט תִּפָּדֶה, וְשָׁבֶיהָ בִּצְדָקָה. (Isaiah 1:27)	ה...
צ	צִיּוֹן יִשְׁאָלוּ דֶּרֶךְ הֵנָּה פְנֵיהֶם, בֹּאוּ וְנִלְווּ אֶל יהוה, בְּרִית עוֹלָם לֹא תִשָּׁכֵחַ. (Jeremiah 50:5)	ח...
צ	צַר וּמָצוֹק מְצָאוּנִי, מִצְוֹתֶיךָ שַׁעֲשֻׁעָי. (Psalm 119:143)	י...
ק	קַמְתִּי אֲנִי לִפְתֹּחַ לְדוֹדִי, וְיָדַי נָטְפוּ מוֹר וְאֶצְבְּעֹתַי מוֹר עֹבֵר עַל כַּפּוֹת הַמַּנְעוּל. (Song of Songs 5:5)	ל...

ק...ן	קוֹלִי אֶל יהוה אֶזְעָק, קוֹלִי אֶל יהוה אֶתְחַנָּן. (Psalm 142:2)	
ק...ת	קָרוֹב אַתָּה יהוה, וְכָל מִצְוֺתֶיךָ אֱמֶת. (Psalm 119:151)	
ר...ה	רִגְזוּ וְאַל תֶּחֱטָאוּ אִמְרוּ בִלְבַבְכֶם עַל מִשְׁכַּבְכֶם, וְדֹמּוּ סֶלָה. (Psalm 4:5)	
ר...ל	רְאוּ עַתָּה כִּי אֲנִי אֲנִי הוּא, וְאֵין אֱלֹהִים עִמָּדִי, אֲנִי אָמִית וַאֲחַיֶּה, מָחַצְתִּי וַאֲנִי אֶרְפָּא, וְאֵין מִיָּדִי מַצִּיל. (Deuteronomy 32:39)	
ר...ן	רְאֵה זֶה מָצָאתִי, אָמְרָה קֹהֶלֶת, אַחַת לְאַחַת לִמְצֹא חֶשְׁבּוֹן. (Ecclesiastes 7:27)	
שׂ...א	שַׂמֵּחַ נֶפֶשׁ עַבְדֶּךָ, כִּי אֵלֶיךָ אֲדֹנָי נַפְשִׁי אֶשָּׂא. (Psalm 86:4)	
שׂ...ה	שְׂאוּ יְדֵכֶם קֹדֶשׁ, וּבָרְכוּ אֶת יהוה. (Psalm 134:2)	
שׁ...ח	שָׁמַע יהוה תְּחִנָּתִי, יהוה תְּפִלָּתִי יִקָּח. (Psalm 6:10)	
שׂ...י	שָׂנֵאתִי הַשֹּׁמְרִים הַבְלֵי שָׁוְא, וַאֲנִי אֶל יהוה בָּטָחְתִּי. (Psalm 31:7)	
שׁ...ל	שָׁלוֹם רָב לְאֹהֲבֵי תוֹרָתֶךָ וְאֵין לָמוֹ מִכְשׁוֹל. (Psalm 119:165)	
שׁ...ם	שְׁמָר תָּם וּרְאֵה יָשָׁר, כִּי אַחֲרִית לְאִישׁ שָׁלוֹם. (Psalm 37:37)	
שׂ...ן	שִׂיתוּ לִבְּכֶם לְחֵילָה פַּסְּגוּ אַרְמְנוֹתֶיהָ, לְמַעַן תְּסַפְּרוּ לְדוֹר אַחֲרוֹן. (Psalm 48:14)	
שׂ...ר	שְׂפַת אֱמֶת תִּכּוֹן לָעַד וְעַד אַרְגִּיעָה לְשׁוֹן שָׁקֶר. (Proverbs 12:19)	
שׁ...ת	שִׁיר הַמַּעֲלוֹת הִנֵּה בָּרְכוּ אֶת יהוה כָּל עַבְדֵי יהוה, הָעֹמְדִים בְּבֵית יהוה בַּלֵּילוֹת. (Psalm 134:1)	
ת...ה	תַּעֲרֹךְ לְפָנַי שֻׁלְחָן נֶגֶד צֹרְרָי, דִּשַּׁנְתָּ בַשֶּׁמֶן רֹאשִׁי, כּוֹסִי רְוָיָה. (Psalm 23:5)	
ת...י	תּוֹצִיאֵנִי מֵרֶשֶׁת זוּ טָמְנוּ לִי, כִּי אַתָּה מָעוּזִּי. (Psalm 31:5)	
ת...ם	תְּנוּ עֹז לֵאלֹהִים עַל יִשְׂרָאֵל גַּאֲוָתוֹ, וְעֻזּוֹ בַּשְּׁחָקִים. (Psalm 68:35)	

Appendix 2: Review Suggestions

As students begin Book 3: עֲמִידָה, they are entering their second year of this prayer program. Just as it is necessary to review basic decoding skills, students will also need to review the prayer texts they studied previously in order to maintain their fluency. Since the ability to join in and lead services are the ultimate objectives of this program, participating in school services is an essential part of any review.

Two review structures are suggested. First, students can review the prayers studied previously by systematically reviewing them in the order which they were taught. This will help students to master the order of the worship service. Conversely, it may be desirable to review those prayers taught previously thematically. In this way the various concepts found within each prayer would receive additional reinforcement. In the same way, holiday blessings would be reviewed as specific holidays occur.

The list below suggests specific prayers from Books 1 and 2 of the זְמַן לִתְפִלָּה Program that share themes with each blessing of the עֲמִידָה. At the same time, prayers that are not taught in this program, but which share themes with blessings from the עֲמִידָה are also noted for possible instruction.

INTRODUCTION: אֲדֹנָי שְׂפָתַי תִּפְתָּח
Prayer to Review: בָּרְכוּ
Common Theme: Praising God.
Other Prayers on This Theme:
מַה־טֹּבוּ, הַלֵּל, בָּרוּךְ שֶׁאָמַר

CHAPTER 1: אָבוֹת
Prayers to Review: שֶׁעָשָׂה נִסִּים, אֲדוֹן עוֹלָם
Common Theme: Our God is the God of history.
Other Prayers on This Theme:
אֵל אָדוֹן, עֶזְרַת אֲבוֹתֵינוּ

CHAPTER 2: גְּבוּרוֹת
Prayers to Review:
מִי־כָמֹכָה, אֱמֶת וְיַצִּיב, אֱמֶת וֶאֱמוּנָה
Common Theme: God helps those in need.
Other Prayers on This Theme:
בִּרְכוֹת הַשַּׁחַר and אַשְׁרֵי

CHAPTER 3: קְדֻשַּׁת הַשֵּׁם / קְדֻשָּׁה
Prayer to Review: אֵין כֵּאלֹהֵינוּ
Common Theme: God is unique.
Other Prayers on This Theme:
אֵין אַדִּיר (מִפִּי אֵל)
On the related theme that God makes us special:
בִּרְכוֹת הַמִּצְוֹת

CHAPTER 4: קְדֻשַּׁת הַיּוֹם
Prayers to Review:
Shabbat blessings, including הַבְדָּלָה / קִדּוּשׁ
Common Theme: Shabbat is special.
Other Prayers on This Theme:
לְכָה דוֹדִי, שָׁלוֹם עֲלֵיכֶם, זְמִירוֹת

CHAPTER 5: בַּקָּשׁוֹת
This chapter summarizes the thirteen intermediate blessings, with thirteen different themes of the weekday עֲמִידָה. Various prayers might be reviewed or taught based on these themes. For example, when teaching the blessing שׁוֹמֵעַ תְּפִלָּה, with its theme that God hears our prayers, it is appropriate to review the שְׁמַע, its theme being that we hear God. Similarly, when teaching the blessing for healing, it might be appropriate to teach the מִי שֶׁבֵּרַךְ.

CHAPTER 6: עֲבוֹדָה
Prayer to review: וְאָהַבְתָּ
Common Theme: Service = love for God.
Other Prayers on This Theme:
יַעֲלֶה וְיָבֹא (which serves as a bridge between

the קְדֻשַּׁת הַיּוֹם and עֲבוֹדָה blessings on festivals, also recalling the service in the ancient Temple).

CHAPTER 7: הוֹדָאָה
Prayers to review:
בִּרְכוֹת הַנֶּהֱנִין, מַעֲרִיב עֲרָבִים, יוֹצֵר אוֹר
Common Theme:
We should thank God for "every day" miracles.
Other Prayers on This Theme:
מוֹדֶה אֲנִי, שׁוֹכֵן עַד

CHAPTER 8: שָׁלוֹם רָב
Prayer to review: הַשְׁכִּיבֵנוּ
Common Theme:
God will bless & shelter us with peace.
Other Prayers on This Theme: תְּפִלַּת הַדֶּרֶךְ

CHAPTER 9: שִׂים שָׁלוֹם
Prayers to review: אַהֲבַת עוֹלָם

Common Theme:
God does wonderful things for us.
Other Prayers on This Theme: בִּרְכַּת הַחֹדֶשׁ

CHAPTER 10: אֱלֹהַי נְצוֹר
Prayer to review: אַהֲבָה רַבָּה
Common Theme: Through the study of תּוֹרָה and perfomance of מִצְוֹת we learn how to lead a life of great value.

A Final Prayer to Teach: מָגֵן אָבוֹת
At the conclsion of teaching the עֲמִידָה, it may be desirable to teach the מָגֵן אָבוֹת, a prayer that summarizes the Shabbat Evening עֲמִידָה, and was added to the service at a time when synagogues were built outside the city walls. By adding this "repetition" of the Shabbat evening עֲמִידָה, latecomers would not be forced to walk home alone. Because מָגֵן אָבוֹת is chanted aloud in many communities, it is certainly appropriate to teach it as a thematic wrap-up to the עֲמִידָה.

Bibliography

Theology

Blumberg, Sherry S. "The Challenge of Teaching About God." In *The New Jewish Teachers Handbook*, edited by Audrey Friedman Marcus and Raymond A. Zwerin. Denver, CO: A.R.E. Publishing, Inc., 1994.

Gellman, Marc, and Thomas Hartman. *Where Does God Live? Questions and Answers for Parents and Children*. New York: Ballantine Books, 1991.

Haberman, Joshua O., ed. *The God I Believe In*. New York: The Free Press, 1994.

The Jewish Education News. Special Focus: God and Spirituality. Vol. 16, No. 1 (Winter 1995).

Kushner, Harold. *When Children Ask about God*. New York: Schocken Books, 1976.

Schulweis, Harold M. *For Those Who Can't Believe: Overcoming the Obstacles To Faith*. New York: HarperCollins Publishers, Inc., 1994.

Sonsino, Rifat, and Daniel B. Syme. *Finding God: Ten Jewish Responses*. New York: UAHC Press, 1986.

Wolpe, David J. *Teaching Your Children about God*. New York: Henry Holt and Company, 1993.

Siddurim

Gates of Prayer for Shabbat and Weekdays: A Gender Sensitive Prayerbook, edited by Chaim Stern. New York: Central Conference of American Rabbis, 1994.

Gates of Prayer: The New Union Prayer Book for Weekdays, Sabbaths, and Festivals. New York: Central Conference of American Rabbis, 1975.

Shilo Prayer Book. 6th ed. New York: Shilo Publishing House, Inc., 1972.

Siddur Pata'h Eliahou: Rituel de Prières Rite Sepharade. Paris: Les Éditions Colbo, 1978.

Sabbath and Festival Prayer Book (Silverman Siddur). New York: The Rabbinical Assembly of America and the United Synagogue of America, 1946, 1973.

Siddur Sim Shalom: A Prayerbook for Shabbat, Festivals and Weekdays, edited by Rabbi Jules Harlow. New York: The Rabbinical Assembly of America and the United Synagogue of America, 1985.

Siddur Sim Shalom: A Prayerbook for Shabbat and Festivals. New York: The Rabbinical Assembly of America and the United Synagogue of America, 1998.

General Prayer

Brown, Steven M. *Higher & Higher*. New York: United Synagogue of America, 1979.

Compass: New Directions in Jewish Education. Special Focus: Tefilah in School. Vol. 17, No. 2 (Summer 1995).

Elbogen, Ismar. *Jewish Liturgy: A Comprehensive History*. Philadelphia: The Jewish Publication Society of America and The Jewish Theological Seminary of America, 1993.

Garfiel, Evelyn. *Service of the Heart*. North Hollywood, CA: Wilshire Book Co., 1978.

Hammer, Reuven. *Entering Jewish Prayer: A Guide To Personal Devotion and the Worship Service*. New York: Schocken Books, 1994.

Idelsohn, A. Z. *Jewish Liturgy and Its Development.* New York: Schocken Books, 1932.

Isaacs, Ronald H. *Lively Student Services: A Handbook of Teaching Strategies.* Hoboken, NJ: KTAV Publishing House, Inc, 1995.

Kadden, Bruce, and Barbara Binder Kadden. *Teaching Tefillah: Insights and Activities on Prayer.* Denver, CO: A.R.E. Publishing, Inc., 1994.

Kadushin, Max. *The Rabbinic Mind.* New York: Bloch Publishing Co., 1972.

Kelman, Stuart, and Joel Lurie Grishaver. "Of Prayer and Pirocess: One Model for Teaching Jewish Prayer." In *The New Jewish Teachers Handbook*, edited by Audrey Friedman Marcus and Raymond A. Zwerin. Denver, CO: A.R.E. Publishing, Inc., 1994.

Kimmelman, Reuven. "The Blessings of Prayerobics." *The B'nai Brith International Jewish Monthly*, Vol. 100, No. 6 (February 1986).

Millgram, Abraham E. *Jewish Worship.* Philadelphia: The Jewish Publication Society of America, 1971.

Nulman, Macy. *The Encyclopedia of Jewish Prayer.* Northvale, NJ: Jason Aronson Inc., 1993.

The Pedagogic Reporter. Special Focus: Siddur, Prayer and Synagogue Skills. Vol. 33, No. 1 (December 1981).

Midrash/Stories

Bialik, Hayim Nahman, and Yehoshua Hana Ravnitzky, eds. *The Book of Legends Sefer Ha-Aggadah: Legends from the Talmud and Midrash.* Translated by William G. Braude. New York: Schocken Books, 1992.

Buber, Martin, ed. *Tales of the Hasidim: Early Masters.* Translated by Olga Marx. New York: Schocken Books, 1947.

———. *Tales of the Hasidim: Later Masters.* Translated by Olga Marx. New York: Schocken Books, 1947.

Frankel, Ellen. *The Classic Tales: 4,000 Years of Jewish Lore.* Northvale, NJ: Jason Aronson Inc. 1989.

Rappoport, Angelo S. *Ancient Israel Myths and Legends.* New York: Bonanza Books, 1987.

Other Resources

Chomsky, William. *Hebrew: The Eternal Language.* Philadelphia: The Jewish Publication Society of America, 1957.

Dobrinsky, Herbert C. *A Treasury of Sephardic Laws and Customs.* Hoboken, NJ: KTAV Publishing House, Inc. and Yeshiva University Press, 1986.

Dori, Rivka. "What We Know about . . . Hebrew Language Instruction." In *What We Know about Jewish Education: A Handbook of Today's Research for Tomorrow's Jewish Education*, edited by Stuart L. Kelman. Los Angeles: Torah Aura Productions, 1992.

Encyclopaedia Judaica. Jerusalem: Keter Publishing House Jerusalem, Ltd., 1972.

The Jewish Education News. Special Focus: Teaching Hebrew. Vol. 18, No. 3 (Fall 1997).

Klepper, Jeffrey. "Af, Peh, Ozen." In *Manginot: 201 Songs for Jewish Schools*, edited by Stephen Richards. New York: Transcontinental Music Publications and New Jewish Music Press, 1992.

Kolatch, Alfred J. *The Complete Dictionary of English and Hebrew Names.* Middle Village, NY: Jonathan David Publishers, Inc., 1984.

Larsen-Freeman, Diane. *Techniques and Principles in Language Teaching.* New York: Oxford University Press, 1986.

Lowin, Joseph. *Hebrewspeak: An Insider's Guide to the Way Jews Think*. Northvale, NJ: Jason Aronson Inc., 1995.

Maiben, Dina. "Issues in Hebrew Reading Instruction." In *The New Jewish Teachers Handbook*, edited by Audrey Friedman Marcus and Raymond A. Zwerin. Denver, CO: A.R.E. Publishing, Inc., 1994.

The Soncino Talmud. London: The Soncino Press, 1960.

Werblonsky, R. J. Zwi, and Geoffrey Wigodor, eds. *The Encyclopedia of the Jewish Religion*. New York: Holt, Rinehart and Winston, Inc., 1966.

Zana, Hillary. "Games and Other Learning Activities for the Hebrew Class." In *The New Jewish Teachers Handbook*, edited by Audrey Friedman Marcus and Raymond A. Zwerin. Denver, CO: A.R.E. Publishing, Inc., 1994.

www.ingramcontent.com/pod-product-compliance
Lightning Source LLC
Chambersburg PA
CBHW081219230426
43666CB00015B/2794